Choosing and Using a
News Alert Service

Robert Berkman
with contributions by Marie Kotas

Published by

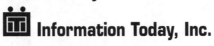 **Information Today, Inc.**

in cooperation with

Find/SVP
Profit From Our Knowledge™

First printing, August 2004

Choosing and Using a News Alert Service

Copyright © 2004 by Information Today, Inc.

Published by
Information Today, Inc.
143 Old Marlton Pike
Medford, NJ 08055-8750
http://www.infotoday.com

in cooperation with

FIND/SVP, Inc.
625 Avenue of the Americas
New York, NY 10011
http://www.findsvp.com

ISBN 1-57387-224-5

Printed and bound in the United States of America.

Publisher: Thomas H. Hogan, Sr.
Graphics Department Director: M. Heide Dengler
Copy Chief: Deborah Poulson
Book and Cover Designer: Ashlee Caruolo

Orders may be placed with Information Today, Inc., by calling (800) 300-9868 or (609) 654-6266 or by visiting our Web site (http://www.infotoday.com).

Table of Contents

Foreword

It seems to be everywhere! No matter where you look another source for news and information appears on the Web. For many Web users it's time-consuming and nothing less than an overwhelming mess. Often it turns into an excuse not to take advantage of one of the things the Internet and electronic research tools can do well, if used properly—allowing the user to "keep current" with the latest news and information from companies, regions of the world, areas of interest, etc., from respected news organizations or directly from company Web sites and watchdog organizations.

Keeping current can not only help you make better and more effective business decisions but might even give you a leg up on your competition.

So, what is a researcher to do? How can you keep current without it becoming an overwhelming, aggravating, and time-consuming experience? The answer for many might be in learning about and making effective use of news alert tools.

In the introduction the author states, "the news alert service arena can be a very confusing one." I couldn't agree more. With so many choices and options I sometimes think that an alert service for alert services is the next step. It seems that on an almost daily basis a new service or technology becomes available.

The good news is that Bob Berkman has assembled a comprehensive, fact-filled, and easy-to-read guide to the many types of news alert services available today in *Choosing and Using a News Alert Service*.

I was very happy to see that this report offers overviews for both free Web-based news alert services and fee-based solutions. This is important since it's very likely that potentially useful material will not be available "on the Web" for free. Also, some fee-based services offer advanced-type functionality that's not available for free.

Berkman also does a terrific job of introducing (and providing useful links) to new and innovative technologies which *are* free or inexpensive and can save you time and effort. He calls them Complementary Alertlike Services. These services include the rapidly growing world of RSS (Rich Site Summary) and a type of tool I use on a daily basis when building my ResourceShelf.com update, Web page monitors.

What's a Web Page Monitor?

Another great service that the free or open Web offers is that in many cases it allows you to go directly to the source of the news. Think about all of the potentially valuable information that never gets reported in the press or is first mentioned on an individual's, company's, or organization's Web site days before it gets mentioned in the news. A Web page monitor allows you to check easily one, ten, or hundreds of different Web sites for changes to their content. It might be a new article posted on the site or it could be something as simple as the removal of a word from a page. In some cases a small change or modification to a page can signal something valuable. Using monitoring software or a monitoring service allows you to review hundreds of pages in a very rapid manner.

I said earlier that trying to keep current with new alert services and tools can also be a challenge. I do my best to monitor what's available, but after reading about the other specialized news alert services included in Chapter 7 I realized that I had not heard of several of the wonderful resources listed there. I think you'll also be impressed.

Take some time to review this report carefully. It offers you an up-to-the-minute guide about the many news alert tools and technologies available today. Using the information included here can not only save you and your organization time and money but can also help avoid information overload, which is something that many of us struggle with these days.

Gary Price, Librarian
Editor, ResourceShelf.com

Introduction

This report is a guide to comparing, choosing, and effectively using a business-focused news alert service. Here, you will learn all about the different types of news alert services, how to make sure you pick the right one for your needs, and how to get the most out of the news alert service you do end up selecting.

The news alert service industry is a hot arena these days, and there are several reasons why this is the case.

First, there's just the sheer *amount* of news now on the Net. The number of online news sources has exploded over the last few years. As of early 2004, nearly all traditional print-based national newspapers from large to small regions have launched some kind of Web-based companion news site. Add to this the even smaller regional newspapers, scores of newswires and online news services, online journals and magazines, niche industry news sites, and, more recently, countless blogs and RSS feeds (RSS feeds are explained on page 2. Furthermore, more and more people are now turning to the Internet as a preferred source for news. According to a 2004 survey conducted by the Pew Internet & American Life, on an average day, 128 million Americans go online to the Internet, and 71 percent of these people get news (www.pewinternet. org/reports/chart.asp?img=Internet_Activities_4.23.04.htm). You can stay up-to-date on new Pew surveys and reports about how Americans use the Internet by linking to www.pewinternet.org/reports/index.asp and via a Pew news alert by linking to http://www.pewinternet.org/signup.asp.

The clear message is that the Internet, as a legitimate or even preferred source for getting the news, has certainly come into its own by 2004.

Why News Alerts?

Today people are increasingly turning to the Net for their news because they want it fast and relevant to their interests, projects, and needs. That's where news alerts come in, as these help solve all of these Net news needs.

Fast: In the age of the Internet, 24-hour cable news, and globalization, what counts the most for many news users—particularly business news users—is speed: how *quickly* you are alerted to the important breaking news. News alerts offer very rapid notification of the latest news (some even offer the ability to get breaking news alerts) right when a new story breaks.

Relevant: Because there is *so much* news on the Net, the hard part for many people is just knowing how to zero in on precisely those news items that are going to be most important and relevant. Since most news alert services (and all of the ones we cover in this guide) allow users to create custom keywords to specify only those topics they want to monitor, news alert services fulfill this need for personalized news delivery as well.

Free: Finally, because news has become a free commodity on the Web, Internet users don't want to have to pay anything to read their news. While there are premium, fee-based news alert services, there are also many quality news alert services that are dirt cheap or absolutely free.

News alerts fill a much sought after need: fast, relevant, and—if need be—free access to the world's news.

A Complex Area

The news alert service arena can be a very confusing one. There are many different kinds of news alert services that cover different types of news sources and are designed for varying markets and customers. Some only monitor news sources on the Web, while others include electronic feeds of print-based publications *not* available freely on the Web. Some are very expensive, some are cheap, and some are free. Some allow advanced keyword search statements and user controls, while others offer only very basic user controls.

One of the primary missions in this guide is to help you sort all of this out—to help clarify just what these news alert services are all about, what kinds of logical categories they fall under, and how to choose the one that best fits your needs.

Here is how we go about this task in this guide.

Scope of This Report

Chapter 1 provides background information so you can put news alert services in a broader context. In this chapter, we'll define what we mean by a news alert service and then provide broad categories for grouping the vendors' different offerings. Here we'll also describe the differences between a news alert service and other types of online current awareness tools (Web page monitors, RSS readers, e-mail newsletters, and table of contents alerts).

Chapter 2 broadly sketches out what we feel would qualify as the best kind of news alert service. Here, you'll be able to review questions that you need to ask yourself to help assess your own specific needs in a news alert service. Then we'll go on to describe what features and qualities a kind of "ideal" news alert service would offer that would be valuable to virtually all users.

Chapters 3 through 6 are the heart of this report, as it is here where you can review detailed feature/price comparisons of more than 20 news alert services and learn how they performed in our hands-on testing. Each of these four chapters covers a different category of news alert services. Chapter 3 compares the free services, Chapter 4 covers very inexpensive alert services, Chapter 5 focuses on the premium, fee-based services, and Chapter 6 separates alerts from what we call "traditional online services" (the major online information vendors that are well-known by librarians and information professionals for the breadth and power of their online databases).

In each of these chapters, we'll provide a brief profile of each service, describe how it performed in a hands-on test, and then provide a detailed table that compares each one's features and pricing to the other alert services within the same category.

What's Included and Excluded?

This guide does not cover every news alert service in existence, so it's worth explaining how we determined which ones to include. Our broad criteria was that to be eligible for inclusion in this report, an alert service would have be of potential value for all kinds of serious news users and researchers, such as librarians, businesspersons, and other professionals—those who want a reliable and powerful method for tracking and being notified of substantive news events.

Specifically, then, we chose those news alert services that:

- Were broad-based—not focused on a particular industry or subject.

- Allowed the user to create his or her own custom keywords to determine precisely what to monitor and track (some alert services only allow users to check off broad categories to monitor: e.g., "sports news," "entertainment news").
- Delivered results directly to the user, either via an e-mail or some other personalized manner.

Ultimately, then, we narrowed our list of relevant news alert services to a final cut of 27 services:

- CBS MarketWatch
- CustomScoop
- CyberAlert
- Dialog: NewsEdge
- Dialog: NewsRoom
- Factiva: Track Module
- FNS: NewsClips Online
- FT.com: Global Media Monitor
- FT.com: News Alerts
- Google News Alert
- Hoover's: News Alerts
- Intelligence Data: InSite 2
- LexisNexis: Personal News
- Luce: CyberClipping
- Luce: FirstAlert
- Moreover: ci-alerts
- Net2one.com
- NetContent: IntelliSearch
- NewsAlert.com
- NewsNow: Online Press Monitoring Service
- NY Times Tracker
- Pinnacor: Inlumen
- PR Newswire: eWatch
- Techdirt
- WebClipping.com
- Yahoo! Alerts
- YellowBrix

Ultimately, from this initial list, we were unable to include five of these alert services: Net2one.com (www.net2one.com), Pinnacor (www.pinnacor.com), Techdirt (www.techdirt.com), FirstAlert (www.burrellesluce.com), and CyberClipping (www.burrellesluce.com). Net2one.com, based in France, did not respond to any of several e-mails and contact attempts. Pinnacor, which produces the Inlumen alert service, was recently purchased by MarketWatch.com. MarketWatch.com informed us that Inlumen is no longer being made available. As we went to press, we were informed that NewsAlert.com was also being discontinued. Techdirt, we ultimately determined, operates in a different manner than a standard news alert service—the firm uses human intelligence to analyze incoming news—so we did not cover it in this report. In addition, while WebClipping.com provided us with data for our comparison charts, it was unable to accommodate our test searching.

And as we went to press, Luce was purchased by Burrelle's and discontinued Luce's FirstAlert and CyberClipping products and introduced two new alerts: NewsAlert and WebClips. While we were unable to test these new alerts, we have been able to include feature and pricing data on them in our feature comparison charts.

Note, too, that after we had completed our tests, we came upon a couple of other news alert services that we felt were notable and should be included in this guide: Nexcerpt and HighBeam. We covered these in a separate profile within their category.

To get the most out of a news alert service, you not only need to choose the right one, but you will also want some strategies on how to make the alert service work well for you. Chapter 7 is devoted to providing you with tips and pointers so that the alert service is going to do what you want it to do. Here we will examine how to create the most powerful and relevant search statement, how to evaluate your results for credibility and usefulness, and how to best integrate incoming news alerts into your daily workflow. We will pay particular attention on how to avoid one of the banes of subscribing to a news alert service—news overload!

The main body of this report wraps up in Chapter 8, where we round out the discussion of news alert services by briefly highlighting specialized and unique alert services not covered in the main guide. These are special purpose alerts that monitor specific types of news developments, ranging from patent filings, to just published market research reports, SEC filings, and more.

This guide concludes with an Appendix that lists approximately 150 "core" business news sources and tables that identify which news alert service includes what title. This Appendix not only identifies which alert services cover key business news sources, but it also can serve as a handy checklist for perusing the names of important business news sources to see which ones you'd like to be able to read regularly (or at least obtain ready access to).

How Our Top Selections Were Chosen

For many of you, the most important part of this report will be our selections of top-ranked news alert services. We have actually made several selections for each of the four broad categories: free, cheap, premium, and traditional. There are cases of more than one selection within the same category as well, reflecting when a different alert service is best suited for a specific application and use.

These selections were based primarily on the results of how the service performed in a few test alerts that were created, as well as by comparing their features and prices. Specifically, here's what we looked for in making final determinations.

Hands-On Test Performance

- How easy was it to navigate the keyword profile creation page?
- How easy was it to create keywords?
- What kinds of power search options were offered?
- Were useful limits and filters available to help make the alert more precise?
- Was ready and relevant help available in creating a search?
- Were there good options and choices in creating preferences in areas like format and frequency of delivery?
- Were relevant results actually received?
- Were there many duplicates?
- Did the e-mails arrive in a reliable fashion?
- Was the e-mail alert itself easily readable and useful?

Sources/Features/Pricing

- Were high-quality business news sources included?
- Were the sources Web-only, non-Web, or a combination of the two?
- Did the service include a wide range of information sources, such as blogs, multimedia, and discussion groups?
- How expensive was the alert service?
- Does it seem like a good value for the money?

Intangibles

- Was the vendor knowledgeable and helpful?
- Were the experiences with the firm's customer service department positive or negative?

Our Top Selections

Here is an up-front summary of the top picks for the news alert services tested:

Free News Alert Services
Google News Alerts

Cheap and Inexpensive News Alert Services
NetContent: IntelliSearch
      Special Mention: HighBeam

Premium, Fee-Based News Alert Services
Dialog: NewsEdge
PR Newswire: eWatch
      Special Mention: Nexcerpt

Traditional Online News Vendors' News Alert Services
Factiva: Track
LexisNexis: Personal News

Chapter 1

Background

What Is a News Alert Service?

Although there are many different levels, types, and variations of news alerts, each one covered in this guide:

- Scans and indexes the full text of a preset number of digital news sources.
- Searches those sources for specific articles/items that match the subscriber's keywords.
- Automatically alerts subscribers to those new news items.

Within the larger umbrella of news alert services, though, there are many variations. The most important ways that alert services vary are:

- **Cost:** Some news alert services are free, some are very inexpensive, and others are quite expensive.
- **Availability:** Some news alert services are available to anyone; others are only available to current clients of the vendor's fee-based online subscription service.
- **Source Type:** Some news alert services index only sources that are available on the open Web, others bypass the Web and index electronic feeds of newspapers and journals delivered directly by the publisher or an aggregator, and some index both pure Web and publisher feeds.
- **Definition of a News Source:** Some vendors have a very broad definition of what is covered by their alert service and may include blogs, message boards, broadcast sites, and industry forums. Others focus more strictly on online newspapers and wire services. Furthermore, some alert services scan several thousand different news sites and sources, while others index a much smaller number.

Other ways that news alert services vary is by targeting a specific audience (typical target audiences include public relations professionals, competitive intelligence professionals, librarians, businesspersons, and general news consumers); by method of delivery (virtually all offer alerts by e-mail, though some offer a Web page for viewing alerts too); and by a wide range of special features and options, which we will discuss later in this report.

Complementary Alertlike Services

News alert services are not the only way to keep track of news and developments on the Web. Other such methods and tools are RSS readers, Web page monitors, e-mail newsletters, and table of contents alert services. While there is some overlap between these various tools, each serves a different purpose. It's worth noting the differences and the function of each of these. A quick Q&A summary of these other monitoring tools follows.

RSS Readers

Q. What is RSS?

A. RSS is an XML-based format that allows Web sites—typically blogs and online news sites—to distribute their content over the Internet via what is called an "RSS feed." Most frequently, that syndicated content is news, broadly defined, meaning it could be general news, or the latest additions to a niche news or blog covering a narrow topic area.

Q. How does RSS work?

A. The RSS feed sent out by the site is automatically parsed into tagged fields: a headline, a short abstract, and a link to the complete story. Anyone with access to an "RSS newsreader," the software used to subscribe to and read RSS feeds, can subscribe and view these feeds. To use an RSS newsreader, you can either download a desktop reader for use on your own PC or link to a site that offers a Web-based RSS reader. Once you have access to an RSS reader, you can go to a news site, look for an icon on the page that indicates that the site owner publishes an RSS feed, and then click on that icon to add that feed for viewing in your RSS readers.

Q. What are some of the main advantages of using RSS?

A. The concept behind RSS is that it makes it easier for users to view headlines and stories of dozens or hundreds of favorite Internet-based news and blog sites all in one place, neatly displayed. Furthermore, users can refresh incoming news stories on a frequent basis in order to view the most recent items posted on those sites.

Q. What are some of the main differences between using RSS vs. a news alert service?

A. There are several key differences. With a news alert service, the vendor, not you, decides ahead of time which news sources to include. A news alert service also normally sends alerts to your e-mail, while RSS readers display all recent headlines, simultaneously on a reader. Also, not all RSS readers allow keyword filtering—normally, you get *everything* that the subscribed-to site publishes. (A couple RSS readers that do offer some keyword filtering are Fastbuzz, www.fastbuzz.com; Feedster, www.feedster.com; and FeedDemon, www.bradsoft.com/feeddemon/index.asp.)

Q. Where can I sign up or learn more?

A. There are lots of free newsreaders around such as AmphetaDesk (www.disobey.com/amphetadesk/) or NewsIsFree (www.newsisfree.com). Another popular newsreader is NewzCrawler (www.newzcrawler.com). You can also get access to a free RSS newsreader by registering with certain Web sites, such as MyWireService (www.mywireservice.com) or Fastbuzz (www.fastbuzz.com).

Web Page Monitors

Q. What is a Web page monitor?

A. A Web page monitor is a piece of software that automatically lets its users know when new text or content has been added to any Web page that the user wants to track.

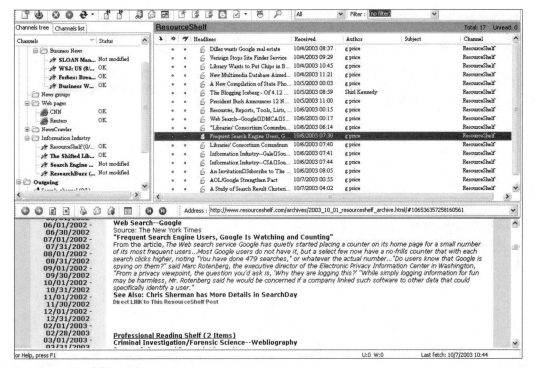

An image of an RSS reader

Q. How does a Web page monitor work?

A. You sign up with a Web page monitor software vendor and then input the URLs of the specific Web pages you want to monitor. Some also permit adding pages on the fly, so as you are browsing the Web and come across a page you'd like to keep track of, you can add it immediately.

Q. What are some of the main advantages of using a Web page monitor?

A. Web page monitors are good for tracking the news and activities of other companies' pages, as well as keeping up with news from favorite sites—especially those that have writers, bloggers, or analysts whose work you like to follow closely.

Q. What are some of the main differences of a Web page monitor vs. a news alert service?

A. News alert services only alert you to new items from news-oriented sites that the alert vendor chooses to include, while a Web page watcher will alert you to any change, from any kind of Web page that you designate.

Q. Where can I sign up or learn more?

A. Link to WatchThatPage at www.watchthatpage.com, TrackEngine at www.track engine.com, or WebSite Watcher at www.aignes.com. WatchThatPage is free and also permits monitoring of pages by keywords. TrackEngine offers a basic level of service for free, and some fee-based add-on premium extras. Note that WatchThat-Page does allow for a very useful word filter, which permits users to filter the changes so that any changes that don't match your keywords are not included in the e-mail alert. WebSite Watcher, which highlights the monitored words on the pages you specify, costs $29.95 but is available for a 30-day free trial.

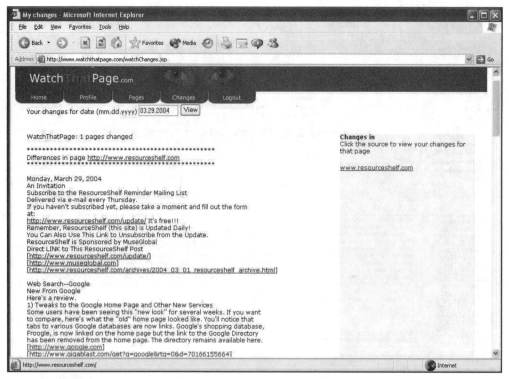

WatchThatPage.com

E-mail Newsletters

Q. What is an e-mail newsletter?
A. It is simply a newsletter in digital form sent to your e-mail.

Q. How does an e-mail newsletter work?
A. Typically, you can subscribe for free, right at the site that offers it.

Q. What are some of the main advantages of using an e-mail newsletter?
A. It is a convenient way to subscribe to a digital publication, particularly if you are already getting much of your news and information online and if the publication contains links to other sites.

Q. What are some of the main differences between an e-mail newsletter and a news alert service?
A. E-mail newsletters do not ask you to create a keyword or specific user profile. Everyone that subscribes receives the exact same information (just like subscribing to a print-based publication).

Q. Where can I sign up or learn more?
A. A listing of substantive business-oriented e-mail newsletters can be browsed at a site that keeps track of new e-letters (and e-zines) called List-A-Day. You can browse

business-oriented e-mail newsletters on that site at list-a-day.com/bizarchives. (In fact, List-A-Day offers its own e-mail newsletter of new e-mail newsletters too!)

Table of Contents Alerts

Q. What is a table of contents alert service?

A. These services simply provide a list of the tables of contents from journals in a particular subject area or group, or from a single publisher.

Q. How does a table of contents alert service work?

A. You sign up with a specialized table of contents vendor or with an individual publisher that makes one available.

Q. What are some of the main advantages of using a table of contents alert service?

A. Rather than reading through all the articles in all of the publications that are of potential interest to you, you can browse their recent tables of contents instead. Then, if you find an article of interest, you can take whatever steps are best to track down the actual article (which could include linking to it on the Web or, if in print, simply getting a print copy at your own library or through an interlibrary loan.)

Q. What are some of the main differences between a table of contents alert service and a news alert service?

A. A table of contents alert service only provides tables of contents, not breaking news.

Q. Where can I sign up or learn more?

A. There are several table of contents alerting services. Below are the names of a few individual publishers that offer a free table of contents alerting service for their own journals:

> **Oxford University Press**
> www3.oup.co.uk/jnls/tocmail/
>
> **Blackwell Press**
> www.blackwellpublishing.com/ealerts/
>
> **SpringerLink**
> www.springerlink.com/app/services/alertingselection.asp?wasp=g2e72jlqvn dyycuq9evl (Focuses on scientific and technical information. Registration required.)
>
> **Sage Publications**
> www.sagepub.co.uk/

If you need to keep up specifically with library literature, we would recommend a free table of contents alert service called The Informed Librarian (www.informedlibrari an.com). You can view the titles of the publications included by The Informed Librarian at www.informedlibrarian.com/ilojnltitles.cfm.

A major *fee-based* alerting service is U.K.-based Ingenta, which previously offered the popular "Uncover Reveal" table of contents alerting service. Users of Ingenta's latest table of contents alerting service can choose to receive tables of contents from a selection of over 28,000 titles indexed by Ingenta. While geared primarily to libraries and institutions, Ingenta also offers a personal user license for individuals who want to obtain a table of contents alert too, for an annual $40 fee (registered users can receive up to five tables of contents for free). To sign up, link to www.ingenta.com/.

	Strictly "News" Monitoring	Delivery via E-mail	Keyword Filters	User Chooses Sources to Monitor
News Alerts	YES	YES	YES	NO
RSS Readers	NO	NO	SOME	YES
Web Page Monitors	NO	VARIES	SOME	YES
E-mail Newsletters	NO	YES	NO	NO
Table of Contents Alerts	NO	YES	RARELY	VARIES

Limitations of News Alert Services

News alert services have certain built-in limitations. They can be a great convenience to help keep you up-to-date if you need to track news on specific companies, products, and issues, but they serve a narrow purpose and should not be your only source of news and information. For one thing, you will obviously never see potentially valuable articles that don't include your keywords. So you still need to try to do some general browsing of the day's papers to stay more generally informed about bigger picture issues.

Furthermore, particularly if you are using a free *Web-only* news alert service, you'll also be missing out on the deeper analytical pieces that are more commonly found in leading business and scholarly publications, which may not make their articles available for free on the Web.

Because news alerts deliver results via e-mail, it is always possible that you'll skip, accidentally delete, or just not have time to read each one as it comes in. That is why you should always have several sources of incoming news as part of your media diet.

A specific flaw, too, that Web-based news alerts suffer from is that sometimes items may be sent to you as new, but they are not new at all. Gary Stock, owner of the excellent Nexcerpt news alert search engine, says that this may happen for a variety of reasons. Some Web sites automatically update their URLs each day, even when there has been no new news, and alert services can be fooled into thinking that the information on the page is fresh. And, says, Stock, sometimes health, how-to, and advisory-type Web sites recycle old material that has been online for a long time as a "new" feature. These items include the current day's date, but in actuality the item has been around for quite some time.

For this reason, you should not automatically assume that items retrieved as new via an alert service were necessarily published that day. If in doubt, you will need to go to the page yourself and examine the article carefully to see if there is an actual byline and date that corresponds to a reputable online news site, or find some other evidence that the new news is truly new!

Chapter 2

What Makes for a Good News Alert Service?

In this guide, you will note that we have given certain news alert services high recommendations. This raises the question: Just what makes for an excellent news alert service? What distinguishes the better ones from the lesser ones?

There are two ways to answer those questions. The first is that, like any product or service, the best news alert service is the one that best matches your own needs. This means that you will need to spend a little time assessing, for yourself, just what it is that you want in a news alert service, and why. We would suggest, then, asking yourself—or surveying your staff if the alert will be going out to a larger group—the following questions.

Broad Questions

- Why am I signing up with a news alert service?
- How do I plan on using the articles when I receive them?
- What am I hoping to get out of using the alert service? How will this help me work better or achieve my work goals?

Narrower Questions

- Do I need to stay up-to-date with general news, broad business news, industry developments? Do I need to track a company, a product, a consumer market, etc.?
- What specific news sources that I rely on and will want to stay on top of are critical?
- Are there news sources that I've heard about and would like access to, but don't currently receive?
- Am I more interested in finding out what is reported in the traditional news press or alternative and cutting edge-type sites? What is being put out over the press wires, or what are people discussing and talking about on the Web?
- Do I need to know about new developments right away? During the same day? Or can the information wait awhile?
- Will I be using these news items for my own purposes, or do I need to get them out to a larger audience? If the latter, will I need to review these news items, comment on them, and put them in a larger context for my audience?

The answers to those questions should provide you with a customized checklist for measuring and assessing competing alert services.

The second way to answer the question of what makes an excellent news service is to recognize that although there is no one perfect news alert service suitable for everyone, it is true that there are certain characteristics and features in a news alert service that have, with few exceptions, qualities that everyone would want in an alert service. Based on our own analysis and testing, we would say that a "perfect" news alert service would integrate as many of these qualities and features as possible.

Deep, Authoritative Business Coverage

The best alert services don't include only newswires and mainstream news sites—these sources have become commodities and can be found anywhere for free on the Web. Instead, the best of the general news alert services include deeper, analytical, and cutting-edge business sources (such as the print-based ones included in the Appendix).

The ideal alert service also integrates many non-U.S. sources so that its users can truly get an international perspective and obtain reports from media sources around the globe.

The best alert services integrate as many different *types* of news sources as possible, drawing from the Internet as well as from electronic feeds of leading business, trade, and academic journals and from top information providers like Gale or ProQuest. When drawing from the Internet itself, the best alert service would include online newspapers, newswires, and journals; selected blogs, Wikis, and RSS feeds; audio and video clips; online discussion groups from Usenet; Web-based forums (like Yahoo! Groups); mailing lists (e.g., Listservs); and any other Web source that is a potential and legitimate tool for new substantive news.

What about breadth of source coverage? If your topic is obscure, the best alert services will be those that have the most sources, since the more sources scanned, the better the chances that news will be located on your topic(s).

Powerful Keyword Search Options

Because the success of your news alert profile will depend to a great degree on the quality and effectiveness of your specific search statement, the ideal alert service will permit you to utilize as many of these advanced search functions as possible:

- Full Boolean searching
- Ability to use NEAR or proximity operators
- Ability to narrow a search by certain segments or "fields." The most important ones are:
  - Title/headline of the news item
  - Specific source title or group of sources
  - Geographic/regional origin of sources

Some of the very sophisticated alert services—primarily those that we have grouped under the "traditional" online vendor category—offer even more filters, allowing users to restrict their search by date of publication, author's name, words in an abstract, and detailed subject codes.

Flexible Format and Delivery Controls

There are several ways to set up and receive alerts, and the best ones offer lots of options so their subscribers can choose exactly how they will receive them. Ideally, users should be able to choose from these options:

- Format: Delivery in plain text or HTML (a few offer XML or even wireless delivery).
- Frequency: Real-time/immediate, hourly, a few times per day, or once per day.
- Article segments: You should be able to choose whether you want to view headlines only (with a link to full story), abstract/extracts only (with a link to the full story), or the full text.

Administrative Controls

While not relevant for all users, if you are looking to roll out a news alert service organizationwide, you'll want to check that the vendor makes it easy to integrate its service onto your intranet or internal network or publish to an internal Web page or portal. The best alert services will have flexible administrative controls that allow you to determine which groupings of staffers in your organization receive which alerts and may even let you add your own annotations and commentary to the incoming alerts. Some will even permit you to "brand" the incoming alert with your own label or logo.

Additional Features

The ideal news alert service will also offer:

- A searchable archive of past news items, available for free searching on the fly at your own convenience on the vendor's Web site.
- A convenient method for storing and sorting incoming alerts into folders, and an easy way to search them and retrieve them (you may be able to do this already with your own software or an add-on program).
- The ability to receive images, audio, and video clips.
- Highlighting of your keywords in the abstract and full text so you can quickly view your keywords to see if the surrounding context is relevant.
- Tools such as statistical analyses for monitoring how well your keywords are doing and which news sources are proving to be the most fruitful.
- Human filtering of "noisy" sources, such as online discussion groups, to cull out the obviously less useful items.
- Detailed, well-written, context-sensitive help screens when you are creating your profile.

Customer Support

The best news alert services offer not only online and e-mail support, but telephone support where users can explain issues or problems to an actual person and receive knowledgeable assistance.

Intangibles

The ideal news alert service not only has excellent coverage and powerful and flexible features, but also:

- Has obviously built human intelligence into its service.
- Has an elegant, intuitive, easily understandable interface.
- Sends an alert even when nothing is retrieved, so you know the alert is working properly.
- Works reliably—there are no or few quirks, odd occurrences, or unexplainable problems.

Finally, the best news alert service will, of course, be priced to fit your budget!

It's not likely that you're going to find *all* of these ideal characteristics and features in a single alert service, but you can use this as a checklist to complement your own needs to help you find the one that comes the closest.

How We Tested the News Alert Services

In order to evaluate the performance of these services, we set up a series of test alerts. To evaluate the free news services, we set up two alerts: One was to find news items containing the phrase "market share" AND wifi; the other was to be alerted to any incoming news that simply containing the keyword "Google."

For the fee-based alerts, we had more precise goals, so we set up the following three test alerts:

Alert #1—With this search profile, we wanted to test how well an alert service would perform in locating hard-to-find business information. Our search was to retrieve news items that mentioned a Chinese firm by the name of Galanz, the world's largest manufacturer of microwave ovens. For this alert, we evaluated the services primarily by how many items they located.

Alert #2—This alert was created to determine how well an alert service would understand a precise Boolean search created to ensure that two concepts would be closely related. Our search here was "lipitor" with "market share" employing a NEAR or proximity operator where available, to try to establish a close relationship between the terms. For this alert, we evaluated the services primarily by whether they retrieved articles that contained both terms, and if the terms were closely linked. As it turned out, this alert proved to be too narrowly focused for most of the services, though it was still interesting to note when an article was located.

Alert #3—This alert was created to test whether a user could refine and filter a broad search to avoid getting too many results, and too many irrelevant items. Our goal was to find articles that discussed buying drugs in Canada. Our search here was (Canada OR Canadian) and drugs, and limiting those words, if the vendor permitted, just to headlines. Here we noted whether we received too many irrelevant articles about Canada and drugs.

In addition to performance in these three areas, we also examined each service on a few other important factors that could not be captured in the feature comparison chart: how easy and intuitive it was to create and set up the alerts, and the formatting and usefulness of the e-mail alert itself.

Chapter 3

Free News Alert Services

One nice thing about news alert services is that there are many that are absolutely free—and several of these are excellent too! Here are free alert services that are designed for the serious Internet news reader:

1. American City Business Journals (bizjournals) "Search Watch"
2. CBS MarketWatch "Keyword News Alert"
3. Google News Alerts
4. Yahoo! Alerts

All of the free alert services only monitor Web-based publications, and most of them operate quite similarly. After registering, you create the keywords or phrases you want to track. All the alert services that we have tested here inform you about new articles by e-mailing the results. Typically, you can choose the frequency of delivery—as they come in, once a day, or at more frequent intervals.

Within the category of free alert services, there are some important distinctions. For example, Yahoo! and Google cover all types of news, while CBS MarketWatch and American City Business Journals focus on business news.

To compare and rate these free news alert services, we set up the same two keyword searches for each, reviewed results, and evaluated each one's performance in our test.

Profiles and Test Results

American City Business Journals
www.bizjournals.com

We've always been a big fan of this site, which aggregates content from regional business journals, as it was one of the first to put up substantive and searchable business content on the Web for free. So it was exciting to discover that now we could not only search the text of the 40 plus business journals, but get alerts too.

Test Performance: The alert service did not live up to our expectations. Several of the stories retrieved did not even contain our keywords. Another problem was that even if the Web page had our keywords, our e-mail alert only provided the top-placed headline on that page, which was not the headline to the relevant story, located lower down on that page. Another downside is that since the publications are weekly, the alerts are only delivered on a weekly basis. Finally, we made a couple of efforts to reach a customer service person, but no one ever responded.

Recommendation: Not recommended. We would say this is still a good site for getting regional business news, but not a preferred choice for an alert service.

American City Business Journals

CBS MarketWatch

cbs.marketwatch.com/tools/alerts/

CBS MarketWatch is well-known in the financial and investment community and has become a leader in providing late-breaking business news on the Web. It offers several different types of alert services: stock price/volume alerts, breaking news alert, company news alert (by stock symbol), industry alert (22 industries), news column alert, and its "Keyword Alert" which is the main news alert function.

Coverage is a small but impressive set, as it includes its own CBS MarketWatch News as well as major press wires, FT.com, *The New York Times*, CNET News, and Knight Ridder News.

Test Performance: In our tests, we received many alerts. Typically, there would be an HTML headline, and occasionally a line or two of text. Most were relevant, although as with American City Business Journals, sometimes the story headline we received in the e-mail did not match the story on the page. The content was primarily from business wires.

Recommendation: A pretty good business alert service, though it would be better if it had the capability to limit results to words and phrases found in the headline of the story.

Google News Alerts

www.google.com/newsalerts

Google News Alerts represents yet another new Google feature. It was introduced in August 2003 and is technically still in beta. The way Google's News Alerts works is that your keywords and phrases are run against all of the breaking news that comes into the Google News service from its 4,500 news services. The first Google News Alerts

CBS MarketWatch

query will send you its top 10 matches. On subsequent alerts, it will send you any re-sults that are new to its news database.

Test Performance: We were very impressed with Google News Alerts. We received many results, and virtually all were relevant—primarily because Google News Alerts is one of the few free alert services that lets you limit your keywords to the headline of the article (by the advanced command, intitle: keyword). We also received our alerts from a wide range of news outlets—small newspapers, online news sites, major news sites, and so on. Interestingly, although *The New York Times* News Tracker is now fee-based, Google News Alerts users can still get alerts from the *Times* for free because Google receives some of the *Times'* news.

Recommendation: Excellent choice for a free news alert service. An outstanding fea-ture is the variety of limits that can be invoked, thereby making your search much more precise. These include limit to headline, specific news source (e.g., source: *Fortune*), and country (e.g., location: UK). You'll need to have these prefixes memorized, because the advanced search page is not linked to the News Alerts to do this automatically for you (as it is for the regular Google News page). One small caution is that you cannot rely on Google News Alerts to send you an alert on each and every matching story. A spokesperson at Google told us that "in the event of a very high frequency of stories per hour, we may not send all sources' stories."

Late Breaking News: As we were going to press, Google introduced a "Web Alerts" feature to complement its News Alerts. The difference between "Web Alerts" and "News Alerts" is that the former automatically runs your keywords against Google's regular Web search and sends you an e-mail alert with links to any new results. The News Alerts feature runs keywords against the regular Web index, so this new feature is not

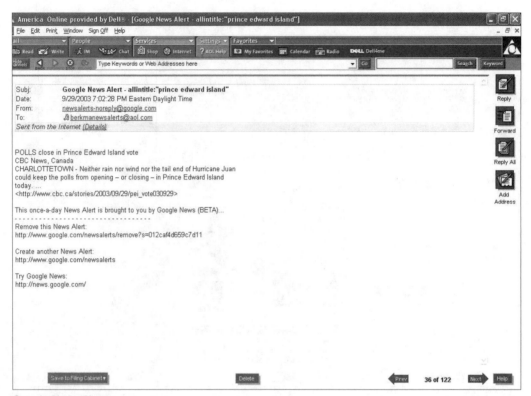

Google News Alert

Yahoo! Alerts

really a way to keep up with new news stories, but a way to automate your search on Google and regularly view the results.

Yahoo! Alerts

alerts.yahoo.com

Yahoo!'s news content is quite good, including not just "the usual suspects" of news and press wires, but solid publications and sites like *The New York Times* (again—free!), *U.S. News & World Report*, Forbes.com, Business Week Online, Adweek.com, *PC World*, and several local newspapers. And, conveniently, you can choose which sources to run your alerts against.

It took several weeks, though, for the Yahoo! service to begin sending alerts, as it apparently had some system problems which are now resolved.

Test Performance: Once we started getting Yahoo!'s alerts, we were very impressed. Each article was relevant and contained a one- to two-line succinct summary of the item.

Recommendation: Apparently, there was an odd quirk in Yahoo!'s system that prevented it from sending the alerts which is unlikely to occur again. So we can heartily recommend Yahoo!, particularly for the quality of its sources and its excellent mini-abstracts.

Feature Comparison: Free News Alert Services					
NAME	Type of Business Content	Advanced/ Boolean Searching	Limits/Filters: H=Headline; G=Geog. Region; N= News Source	Delivery Timing and Options	Other Features
American City Business Journals Search Watch	Regional business journal articles	Phrases: NO Boolean (+sign for must)	G (Cities)	Once per week on Monday	Industry reports Daily business updates
CBS MarketWatch Keyword News Alert	Business-focused Web-based news services, wires, and publications	Phrases; Boolean (AND, OR)	N	Daily; Immediate	Up to 25 alerts permitted Can temporarily "suspend" alerts
Google News Alerts	Breaking News from 4,500 news sources on the Web	Phrases; Boolean	H, G, N (Can also limit words/phrases in URL and by date	Daily; Immediate	Up to 10 alerts Permitted
Yahoo! Alerts	Over 50 online news publications	Phrases; Limited Boolean: Boxes: (must or must not contain)	N	Daily; Immediate	Also: Breaking News Alert (Reuters or AP) Bulletins (headlines by subject category) Can choose to limit to the 10 business-oriented news sources Can receive alerts via Yahoo! Messenger

A New Free Alertlike Service Just for Blogs and RSS

As we were going to press, we came across a very intriguing, specialized alert service called PubSub, which, according to the firm, scans over a million Weblogs and RSS news feeds. Users can input custom keywords to get a link to a specific URL that will regularly provide refreshed listings of new blog and RSS feeds that match the keyword profile with the user's keyword in bold.

Note that unlike the news alerts covered in this report, subscribers to PubSub don't actually get ongoing e-mail alerts each time a new relevant blog or RSS item is detected. Instead, the user receives a URL that can be checked at the user's convenience to browse the latest incoming entries.

One interesting distinction between PubSub and other free alert services is that users are NOT required to provide personal information to register—one just simply inputs the keyword terms and an e-mail address.

For more information, link to www.pubsub.com.

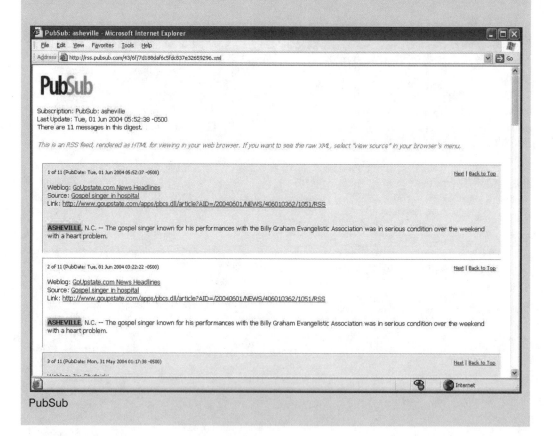

PubSub

Chapter 4

Cheap News Alert Services

Another category of news alerts—and, it seems, an increasingly popular one—are those that are not completely free but are downright bargains. These may cost as little as $29 per year, or as much as $100. Typically, they offer more features and capabilities than the free ones and are more robust. However, unlike the most expensive ones covered in the next section, they are either limited to a single publication or cover only Web sources.

The services we covered here, that we placed into this category, are:

- New York Times News Tracker $19.95/year
- FT. com: News Alerts   £70/year
- NetContent: IntelliSearch $29.95/month

Two new services that we came across late in compiling this guide are listed below. We were unable to provide a full review, but we do cover them briefly.

- HighBeam $19.95/month or $99/year
- Rocketinfo $29/year for personal desktop version

These two additional inexpensive news services are covered in the sidebar on p. 24.

Profiles and Test Results

The New York Times: Times News Tracker
www.nytimes.com/premiumproducts/newstracker/index.html#
New York, NY
The New York Times was founded in 1851. Its alert service was launched in 2002.

Target Market: All news readers.

Key Claims: Get just the essential breaking news based on the editorial judgment of the *Times*.

Special Features: Up to 10 alerts; 90-day archive; dedicated customer service.

For a long time, *The New York Times* had given away its Tracker alert service, but in 2003 it began charging the modest rate of $19.95 per year. In 2004, it raised the rate to $29.95. There is one overriding distinction when considering using the *Times*'s alert service: The content is limited to just one news source—*The New York Times*, of course.

Test Performance: We very much liked using the Times News Tracker—ironically, one reason was precisely *because* we were only monitoring one information source, as

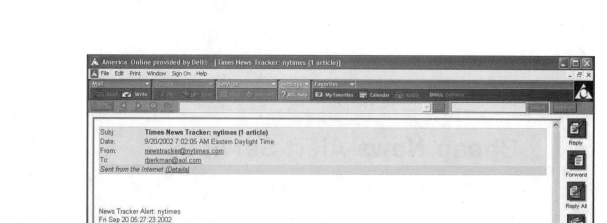

Times News Tracker

it was one that, to us at least, was a trusted source. Furthermore, when we received an alert—and they were always relevant because we could limit our words to the head-line—we could also make the determination that the news item was inherently im-portant and noteworthy *because* it was published in the *Times*.

Recommendation: We'd say the service is worth $29.95 per year. One of the best fea-tures is the capability to run a precision keyword search within a precision-tagged cat-egory, thereby increasing the relevance and value of the alerts.

FT.com: News Alerts
www.ft.com
West London, U.K.
Financial Times newspaper was founded 1888. FT.com was launched in 1996.

Target Market: Businesspeople, including financial executives and business execu-tives with a global focus.

Key Claims: News alerts are included with an FT.com subscription.

Special Features: Company tracking option.

Test Results: No results were obtained on any of the three searches.

Sample Sources: FT.com.

Intuitiveness and Ease of Set Up: Setting up an alert on FT.com was extremely sim-ple and very intuitive.

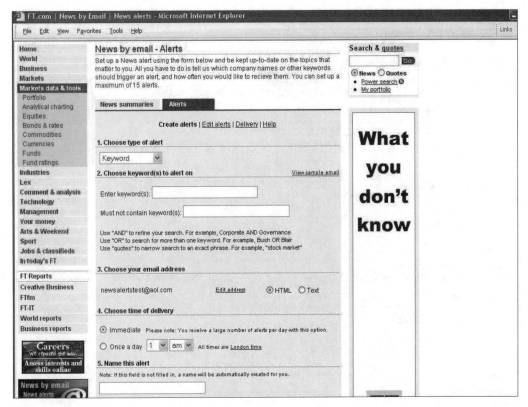

FT.com

Comments: You cannot limit to headline only; you can, though, use a "PowerSearch" form to utilize broad industry, region, and topic filters. No more than 15 alerts are permitted. The e-mail alerts contain the full article and are very nicely formatted and easy to read.

Bottom Line: This is a great choice if you are a fan of the *Financial Times*, have a fairly broad search, and want to know how this respected site and international newspaper covers your topic. But as evidenced by our own test searching, your source set is limited to one news site (though subscribers can still run on-the-fly searches on the site that search multiple news sources). This alert would be of particular value for tracking European and international companies and subjects.

NetContent: IntelliSearch
www.netcontentinc.net
Nashville, TN
Founded 1999

Target Market: All types of researchers in businesses and organizations.

Key Claims: Retrieves content from the invisible Web.

Special Features: Low-cost, multiuser packages, 14-day free trial, limit by region or source type.

Test Results: No results were retrieved on our first two alerts. On Alert #3, many results were retrieved and the majority were relevant.

NetContent: IntelliSearch

Sample Sources: *Knight Ridder/Tribune Business News, Charleston Gazette, Drug Week, St. Louis Post Dispatch, Web Content, Tulsa World, Canada NewsWire.*

Intuitiveness and Ease of Set Up: Excellent.

Comments: IntelliSearch offers quality sources from the Web and very nice filtering capabilities by publication, region, and date range. Most impressive were the e-mail alerts themselves, which were clearer than competitors' and provided excellent bibliographies and summaries.

Bottom Line: Although not as powerful as some competitors, and covering fewer sources, for the money, IntelliSearch is an excellent value and highly recommended.

When scanning the chart on p. 21, compare these important factors:

Coverage: In general, the more sources the better. Look also at the data for international coverage.

Type of Sources: The most common sources are digital newspapers and newswires. Some vendors also include electronic versions of print papers and trade journals, and some include online discussion groups and blogs.

Information Providers: In this category, we have listed the most sought after and premium business information providers. Only a few alert services include one or more of these suppliers.

User Controls: To avoid news alert overload, it is very important to be able to limit one's keywords to a source's title/headline, and, if possible, by individual source and/or geographic region.

Delivery: Virtually all alert services can provide the alert either by e-mail or on a Web site. A few offer extra features like wireless delivery or XML. Most allow the users to choose to obtain their alerts either on a continuous basis or on a predetermined time, such as once or twice a day. Another difference is in what you receive—while most provide a headline and abstract, some services only provide a headline.

Intranet Use: Do you want to integrate an alert service onto your intranet? Some vendors not only allow this, but also offer various administrative controls. Some will even let the client integrate its own internal news and announcements with the alert service.

Archive: The availability and length of an alert service's archive can vary quite a bit, as well as whether the archive is even searchable.

Special Features: A few alert services offer extras such as images, or some level of data analysis or manipulation.

Pricing: A wide range of pricing schemes is made available from alert firms.

Customer Support: Easily available and quality telephone customer support is important for alert service users. Some offer such support 24 hours per day, 7 days a week, but most have more limited hours.

Here are explanations for the abbreviations and protocols used in the chart that follows:

Type Sources: A count for each type of source was provided where the vendor was able to supply the data. Sources that the vendor informed us were emphasized are highlighted in bold text.

User Controls: Limit alerts by: Headlines (H), Source Titles (S), Geographic Region (R).

Delivery/Frequency: D=Daily, 2/D=Twice per day, 3/D=Three times per day, H=Hourly, W=Weekly, M=Monthly, Immed.=Immediately/Continuously.

Feature Comparison: Inexpensive News Alert Services

	New York Times Times News Tracker	FT.com News Alerts	NetContent IntelliSearch	HighBeam Elibrary*	Rocketinfo RocketNews Enterprise
Coverage --No. Sources	1:*The New York Times*	1: *Financial Times*	9,000	2,600	10,000[1]
--International			20%	15% (includes a small number of French and Spanish titles)	35% (and can search any Germanic Characters
--Restricted to Web Souces	NO	NO	NO	NO	YES
Type Sources --Newswires	NO	NO	YES	YES	YES: 250
--Print Papers	YES: 1	YES: 1	YES	YES	NO
--Online Papers	YES: 1	YES: 1	YES	NO (W)	YES: 7,000
--Journals	NO	NO	YES	YES	YES: 1,750
--Usenet	NO	NO	NO	NO (W)	On Request
--Listservs	NO	NO	NO	NO	On Request
--Blogs	NO	NO	YES	NO (W)	See note 1
--Co.	NO	NO	YES	NO (W)	On Request

	New York Times Times News Tracker	FT.com News Alerts	NetContent IntelliSearch	HighBeam Elibrary*	Rocketinfo RocketNews Enterprise
Directories					
--Mkt. Res. Rep	NO	NO	YES	NO (W)	YES: 250
--Invest. Reports	NO	NO	YES	NO	YES: 250
--Other	NO	NO	NewsNow, RSS Feeds	Maps, photos, images, transcripts, government articles, hearing transcripts, reference works (encyclopedias, dictionaries, almanacs, books— great works of literature)	Radio and television transcripts
Providers Include					
--DJ/Factiva	NO	NO	NO	NO	YES
--Proquest	NO	NO	YES	YES	NO
--Gale	NO	NO	YES	YES	NO
--Hoover's	NO	NO	NO	NO	NO
--Knight Ridder	NO	NO	YES	NO	YES
--RDS	NO	NO	NO	NO	NO
--Other	NO	NO	NewsNow	NO	Bloomberg, Reuters
User Controls					
--No. of Alerts Allowed	10	15	Unlimited	15 (25 full members)	Based on license
--Limit Alerts by	H**	None	T, R	H, T (only 1), +author/date	H^2, T^3, R^3
--Boolean Searches	YES: Phrases; All/Any/ None pull-down choices	YES: AND, OR, "phrase"	YES: Including NEAR/ Proximity	YES: Phrases; AND, OR, NOT (natural language also permitted)	YES: Including NEAR/ Proximity
--On-the-Fly Searching Permitted	YES	YES	YES	YES	YES
Delivery/ Frequency					
--Method	E-mail	E-mail	E-mail, Web	E-mail	E-mail, Web[4]
--Frequency	D, Immed.	D, Immed.	D	D, W	D, W, H, Immed.
--Real Time	YES	Short Delay	NO	NO	YES
Intranet Use					
--Available	NO	NO	YES	NO	YES
--Admin. Controls	NO	NO	YES	N.A.	YES

	New York Times Times News Tracker	FT.com News Alerts	NetContent IntelliSearch	HighBeam Elibrary*	Rocketinfo RocketNews Enterprise
--Ability to Integrate Firm's Own Internal News	NO	NO	YES	N.A.	YES
Archive --Available	YES	YES	YES	YES—28 million documents	YES
--Backfile	1 week/Free Jan. '96+/Fee	5 years	1 year	20 years	6 months
--Searchable	YES	NO	YES	YES	YES
Special Features --Images --Analysis --Other	NO NO Can also choose a "Topic" alert to match full stories Can choose one of four e-mail delivery time ranges	NO NO Company alerts by ticker symbol	NO NO N.A.	1 million+ NO See Sidebar on page 24	NO NO Can annotate incoming alerts with notes and comments
Pricing --Subscription Fee	$29.95/yr.	Included in FT.com level one pricing (£70/yr.)	$29.95/mo.	$19.95/mo. or $99.95/yr. ***	$6,000/yr.+ based on license
--Other Fees	NONE	NONE	NONE	NONE	NONE
Customer Service --Phone Support --Hours/Times	YES 9 A.M.–5 P.M. (M–F)	YES 8 A.M.–midnight U.K. time	YES 8 A.M.–5 P.M. CST (M–F)	YES 9 A.M.–6 P.M. CST (M–F)	YES 6 A.M.–9 P.M. (M–F)

* HighBeam is split into two major sections: "Elibrary," a traditional database consisting of electronic versions of thousands of trade journals and other substantive information sources, and "Web," which segments information on the Web into several categories (online news, search engines, discussion groups, and other areas) and allows users to search Web-only sources. The data provided in the chart applies only to the Elibrary portion of the service, since this is the portion for which users may specify alerts. However, we have used a "W" to indicate where users can obtain information from the Web by doing a search on the HighBeam site, but may not receive actual alerts.

** Can also limit to specific byline, and to words that appear in specific sections of *The New York Times*.

*** Registered users can search HighBeam for free, but not view the full text of articles, set up alerts, or use other special features.

Rocketinfo

1. At press time, Rocketinfo told us they were planning on adding 80,000 Weblogs and RSS feeds in the next version of the product.
2. Can limit to words in headline alone or headline and excerpt.
3. Set up by firm for client.
4. Also can deliver to wireless device.
5. Inexpensive desktop version available without alerting and other capabilities.

Two New and Unusual Services: Highbeam and Rocketinfo

HighBeam: More Than a Typical News Alert Service

One of the more intriguing additions to the news alert arena is HighBeam Research, an online research site created by Patrick Spain, whose claim to fame is that he is a co-founder of Hoover's as well as being the owner of the popular Elibrary and Researchville research sites.

Elibrary was actually integrated into HighBeam when the service was launched in late January 2004 by Spain's company, Alacritude. At that point, Alacritude changed its own name to HighBeam.

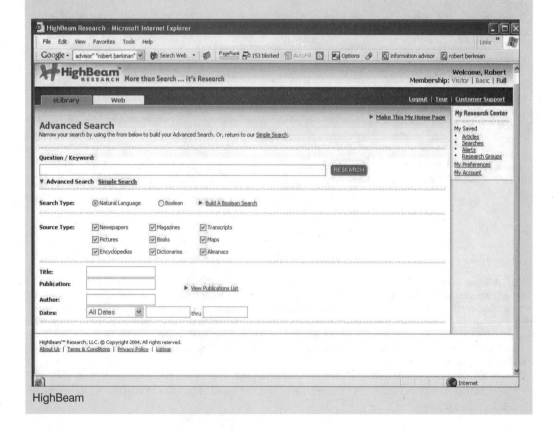

HighBeam

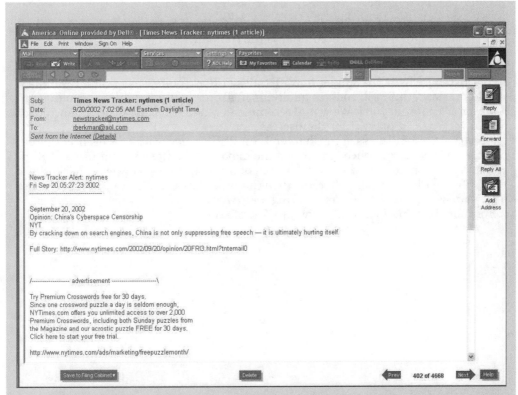

Rocketinfo

Although primarily designed as a publication database and Web metasearch service and not an alert service, HighBeam does includes an alert service as a key feature. The service also offers several capabilities that are unusual and make it stand out from the other competing services, particularly the other inexpensive ones covered in this guide. We'd say that these primary distinctions are as follows:

- Quality of the news sources—the "Elibrary" portion of HighBeam consists of digitized versions of top print business and trade journals not readily available for free on the Web. In total, there are more than 28 million articles and pictures.
- Ability to search and download images.
- Ability to customize Web content into personalized "Research Groups" of custom designated source collections.
- A variety of types of documents such as images, maps, and reference books.
- Ability to select portions of the Web to do more focused Web searching. High-Beam splits the Web into several substantive areas: online news, search engines, discussion groups, and more.

For more information, a full review of the HighBeam Research service can be found in the April 2004 issue of *The Information Advisor*.

Rocketinfo: An RSS Reader with Some Alerting Capabilities

We were very impressed with a recent trial of Rocketinfo, which is primarily an RSS and news aggregation site that operates on one's desktop. Rocketinfo collects and organizes incoming news and groups it into several categories: News Search,

Headlines, Industry, RSS, Weblog, Gartner, IDC, Book Search, Archive. A total of 10,000 sources are scanned, according to the company.

The version available in March 2004 did not offer an alert service, except for a special enterprise edition that delivered results via XML, e-mail, or on a mobile device. Darren DeJean, co-founder and VP Sales at Rocketinfo, says that a revamped version of Rocketinfo will contain additional features and capabilities including an alert service later in 2004. We would recommend readers of this report to download a trial version and to try it for themselves.

Note that as we discussed in Chapter 1, an RSS reader works differently than a standard news alert service, and one of the major distinctions is that users of RSS cannot create an advanced set of keywords to filter the news. However, Rocketinfo does offer a "filter" option whereby *after* the news has come in to the reader, the feeds can be further filtered by entering a keyword.

For more information, link to www.rocketinfo.com.

Chapter 5

Fee-Based/Premium News Alert Services

Our next grouping of news alert services is what we categorize as fee-based and premium services. This group offers the most sophisticated features and controls, and many are suitable for large organizations and for use over an internal network. Signing up for an alert vendor in this category can cost anywhere from $1,500 to $20,000+ per year. Here are the vendors that we have placed under this category:

- Burrelle's/Luce: NewsAlert and WebClips
- CustomScoop
- CyberAlert
- Dialog: NewsEdge
- FNS: NewsClips Online
- FT.com: Global Media Monitor
- Hoover's: News Alerts
- Moreover: ci-alerts
- NewsNow: Media Monitoring Service
- PR Newswire: eWatch
- WebClipping.com
- YellowBrix

Burrelle's/Luce

As discussed earlier in this report, NewsAlert and WebClips from Burrelle's/Luce are new products that became available as a result of the merger between the two firms in October 2003. While it was too close to press time to actually test these two new alert services, the vendor was able to answer all of the questions regarding its features and prices of its NewsAlert product, which is included in the feature comparison chart in this chapter on page 39. (Note that Burrelle's/Luce also offers a chat-only monitoring service called CyberTalk.)

Note, too, that after the hands-on testing of these alert services was completed, we also came across a very unusual and impressive alert service called Nexcerpt, which was reviewed in the March 2004 issue of *The Information Advisor*. See the write up at the end of this chapter for an excerpt from that review.

Profiles and Test Results

CustomScoop
www.customscoop.com
Concord, NH
Founded 2000

Target Market: Public relations professionals.

Key Claims: Covers TV, radio, new media; duplicate story filtering.

Special Features: Free two-week trial; can limit search by state or by one of three sections of a newspaper (sports, obituaries, opinion pages); analysis and reporting options; can download clips in Excel.

Test Results: CustomScoop was able to locate a couple of items on the first two alerts, though an item for #2 included only one of the two terms. CustomScoop performed poorly on search #3, retrieving many irrelevant results.

Sample Sources: *Ft. Worth Star Telegram, Halifax Herald, Financial Times, Salt Lake City Tribune, Durham Herald Sun, Standard & Poor's Personal Wealth.*

Intuitiveness and Ease of Set Up: Very easy to set up, but there were not many advanced search options available.

Comments: CustomScoop searches only Web sources. There was no ability to limit one's search by title/headline, which caused the relevancy problems in Alert #3. On the positive side, the e-mail alerts themselves were cleanly formatted and easy to browse. An interesting feature allowed us to create charts to visually identify where the clips were derived from: both by source type and by specific title.

Bottom Line: A good alert service for very obscure topic monitoring, but not for broad searches.

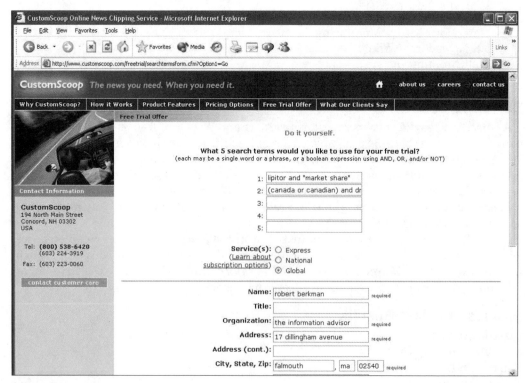

CustomScoop

CyberAlert 4.0
www.cyberalert.com
Stamford, CT
Founded 1999

Target Market: Business-oriented media monitoring; public relations; marketing and brand management; market research; competitive intelligence; investor relations; intellectual property researchers.

Key Claims: No duplicate clips; advanced filtering for better relevancy.

Special Features: Users can "name their own price" by submitting a bid(!); can e-mail and share clips on Web site.

Test Results: For Alerts #1 and #2, CyberAlert found a total of two items, but one was linked to a subscription-only Web site. An enormous number of results were located for search #3; however, a great deal of these were irrelevant.

Sample Sources: *Reuters, Go News, Arabic News, Alternative News Network, Bio-Space, Yahoo! News, Pundit Magazine.*

Intuitiveness and Ease of Set Up: Not applicable, as the alert was set up by a vendor.

Comments: Despite its claims of higher relevancy, the inability to limit an alert to a headline resulted in retrieving many overly broad and irrelevant results in our broader #3 search. We also found the summary e-mails to be a bit confusing and not too intuitive. The results were easier to view when we linked directly to CyberAlert's Web site.

Bottom Line: An okay, but not great, alert service. CyberAlert retrieves information from a wide range of Web sites beyond what one considers typical "news" sites: This will retrieve more results, but not all will be strictly news-type items.

Dialog: NewsEdge
www.newsedge.com
Cary, NC
Founded in 1998 as Desktop Data. Purchased by the Thomson Corporation in 2001, and today is part of Thomson's Dialog group.

Target Market: Market intelligence users in large organizations of all types.

Key Claims: Superior refining technology for filtering relevant breaking news; real-time business information; focus on enterprise applications.

Special Features: Ability to include/exclude press releases; uses industry- and company-specific tags; can include or exclude specific sources.

Test Results: NewsEdge performed the best of all services on Alert #1, retrieving three items. For the broad #3 search, NewsEdge did not retrieve many results, but all were relevant.

Sample Sources: *Wall Street Journal, AP, Financial Times, EIU ViewsWire, Charleston Daily Mail.*

Intuitiveness and Ease of Set Up: It was easy to create a search and alert on NewsEdge, though the various module creation options are a little involved and complex.

Comments: NewsEdge offered a range of advanced search operators and limits, with precision subject tags. There was excellent search help advice and customer service was very knowledgeable and helpful. The e-mail alert itself was particularly well formatted and easy to read and provided a succinct one-line summary of each item. Also nice was NewsEdge's main Web page, which displayed retrieved items in a cleanly republished format. One drawback is that NewsEdge does not provide a mechanism for the removal of duplicates.

Bottom Line: Excellent sources, precision search functions, and customer service. Highly recommended.

FNS: NewsClips Online
news-clips.com
Washington, DC
Founded 1985

Target Market: News media; government agencies; lobbyists; associations; and companies.

Key Claims: Fixed pricing; custom reports.

Special Features: Includes coverage of news, public affairs, sports, government, and other selected television and radio broadcasts for over 150 markets around the U.S.

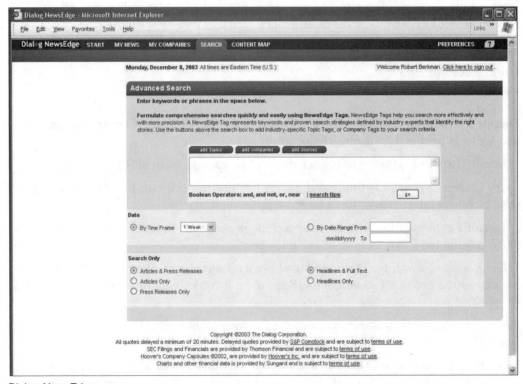

Dialog NewsEdge

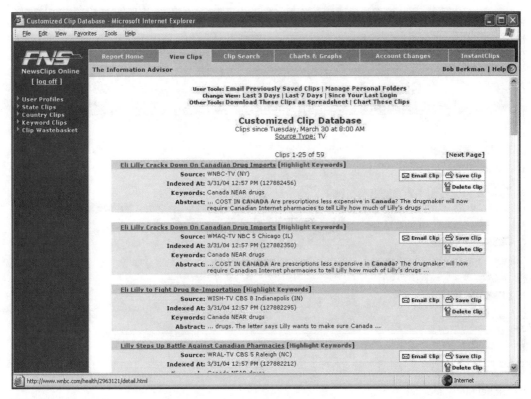

FNS NewsClips

We were unable to complete our tests fully at the same time the other tests were run, but it should be pointed out that NewsClips Online is basically a rebranded version of CustomScoop, though FNS adds and integrates its own television and radio broadcast monitoring service. Users of the service will receive clips that contain a 50-word abstract of relevant broadcast programs and then have the option to order a complete transcript for an additional fee from FNS. (To see how the television and radio monitoring service works, link to fednewsmonitoring.com and click on "free demo.")

FT.com: Global Media Monitor (GMM)

news.ft.com/FTCorporate/Site/html/uk/research/ftpro.html
West London, U.K.
Financial Times newspaper was founded in 1888. The FT.com site was launched in 1996.

Target Market: Business executives.

Key Claims: Covers the world's top media sources; extensive archive.

Special Features: European/International coverage; abstracts of non-English news.

Test Results: One item was retrieved on Alert #1, but nothing on Alert #2. A small number of items were retrieved on Alert #3, but most were not relevant.

Sample Sources: *Fair Disclosure Wire, Asia Africa Intelligence Wire, The Post* (Zambia), *PR Newswire, Corporate Announcements Intelligence Wire, CCN NewsWire, The Economic Times, The Guardian*.

FT Global Media Monitor

Intuitiveness and Ease of Set Up: There are four methods for creating a search: easy, text, Boolean, and power. The first three methods are straightforward, but we found the power search form quite confusing as well as the various "drawers," "attach modes," and other set-up options.

Comments: The e-mail alerts were not very well formatted. We retrieved many irrelevant results on our broader search, which was a result of GMM's inability to limit to a headline search. We did, though, like that the news items we linked to were nicely reformatted into a standard article view.

Bottom Line: We were not particularly impressed with GMM, though it could serve users who need to track non-English language news stories on issues covered in the global press.

Hoover's: E-Mail News Alerts
www. hoovers.com
Austin, TX
Founded 1996. Purchased by Dun & Bradstreet in 2002.

Target Market: Business researchers of all types.

Key Claims: Tracks companies, industries, and people for the business user.

Special Features: Can search/limit by ticker symbol and by specific industry.

Test Results: Hoover's retrieved a couple of items for searches #1 and #2. For the broader #3 search, Hoover's retrieved many items, but we had a major problem with irrelevant news items.

Hoover's E-Mail News Alerts

Sample Sources: *Canada NewsWire, AP, The Times of India, St. Petersburg Times, Liverpool Daily Post, All Africa Global Media.*

Intuitiveness and Ease of Set Up: Hoover's alerts were extremely easy to set up—perhaps too easy, as we could have used more search features and options.

Comments: What we liked best about Hoover's was its solid business sources, the easy set up, a nice interface, and the very clean reformatted results page that included our keywords in bold. There was no search help screen on the alert page, though, so we needed to call customer service for search help. We found its customer service to be quick and friendly, though the representative didn't quite grasp the difference between an AND operator and the use of quotation marks. The e-mails were excellently formatted with full bibliographic information. Hoover's biggest flaw is that it doesn't allow headline limiting, which caused far too many irrelevant results to be retrieved, exacerbated by wire service duplicates. Note that Hoovers offers several levels of subscription options, and you must sign up with the Hoover's "Pro" option (or higher) to be eligible for the alerts.

Bottom Line: A very good alert service, but needs more power search options.

Moreover: ci-alerts

www.moreover.com
San Francisco, CA
Founded 1999

Target Market: Businesspeople: executives, sales, business development, marketing and public relations; R&D; librarians.

Key Claims: Monitors the most influential Internet sites, including message boards; real-time monitoring.

Special Features: Administrative controls, group alerts, subject categorization via human editors, free trial.

Test Results: No items were retrieved on Alerts #1 and #2. Several items retrieved for Alert #3 and all were very relevant, though we did have duplicates until we checked a "remove duplicates" box.

Sample Sources: *Business Week, Reuters, Forbes, Medical Post, iWon, Time, Erie Times, Pharmacy Practice, Bloomberg*.

Intuitiveness and Ease of Set Up: The search form was a little rough and off-putting, but there were some good power search options.

Comments: Although a headline limit is permitted, it could only be performed via a pull-down box, which did not allow us to combine a Boolean with a headline search, so we had to modify our search. There were, however, a date filter, stock ticker filter, and a few hundred predetermined subject filters as well as a country and industry filter. In the e-mail alerts, we did not receive much bibliographic information on our results—only a headline, source name, and URL. We also had a few small technical problems in getting one of the alerts to operate correctly. Note that Moreover is planning to introduce a new version of its alert service.

Bottom Line: A good, but not great, business news alert service.

Moreover

NewsNow: Online Press Monitoring Service

www.newsnow.co.uk
West London, U.K.
Founded 1997

Target Market: PR; marketing; market intelligence; and research departments in medium- to large-size companies.

Key Claims: Tracks over 10,000 Web sites in 600 distinct categories. U.K.'s leading online press monitoring firm.

Special Features: Home page lists breaking news stories in categories, available to anyone. Can deliver to an intranet/extranet or password-protected Web site. Monitors large and small Web sites. Fourteen-day free trial.

Test Results: For Alerts #1 and #2, NewsNow retrieved a few results, and all were relevant. On Alert #3, NewsNow retrieved many results, and virtually all items were relevant.

Sample Sources: *Desert Morning News, The Washington Post, The BostonChannel.com, Dow Jones Newswire, Lycos Finance, WBZ4, Business Week.*

Intuitiveness and Ease of Set Up: Not applicable, as the alert was set up by NewsNow.

Comments: Although NewsNow only monitors Web sites, it offers powerful features such as the ability to limit keywords to the headline, date, and URL. E-mails were nicely formatted but did not offer a substantive abstract or summary. Clicking on the URL in an e-mail redirects the user to the publisher's article with keywords nicely highlighted in yellow. We also very much liked the user's home page, which listed and categorized one's incoming stories based on currency.

Bottom Line: Although limited to the Web, NewsNow is a very good monitoring service, and we would recommend its use.

PR Newswire: eWatch

www.ewatch.com
PR Newswire was founded 1888
eWatch was launched in 1995

Target Market: Public relations professionals; competitive intelligence professionals; business researchers.

Key Claims: Focuses on uncovering media, sites, and people that mention specified firms and products.

Special Features: Monitors online discussion areas including investor boards (for an additional fee); various reports generated; readership data provided for online sites.

Test Results: No results were retrieved for our first two searches. We received several hundred matches for our Canada/drugs alert (we would have preferred fewer, more targeted results, but eWatch did not permit a limit to headline only).

Sample Sources: *The Miami Herald, FT.com, Yahoo! Finance, Reuters, CBSNews.com, Excite, LA Times.*

Intuitiveness and Ease of Set Up: The way eWatch works is that the client describes his or her concepts, keywords, and purpose, and then the search statement is created

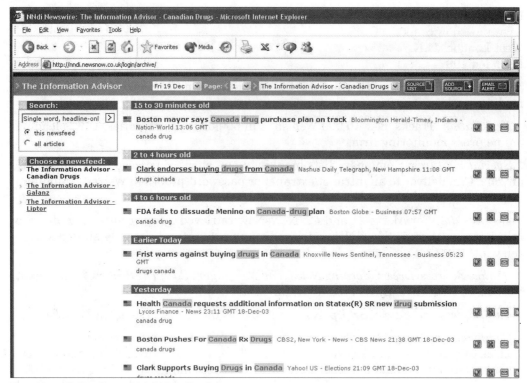

NewsNow: Online Press Monitoring Service

by eWatch's customer service. When we reviewed how our searches were set up, we found that they were done quite well, and included appropriate nested Boolean precision search terms.

Comments: The Web page where clients view recent results is very graphically appealing, and eWatch offers many features and functions not available on other news monitoring services. Among these are highlighted keywords, the ability to easily e-mail articles with an accompanying message, and topic coverage reports. Also, the results list identifies how many times one's keyword(s) appeared in the item and if the listed item is part of a no-subscription, free subscription, or fee-based subscription site. Users can mouse-over abbreviated titles to view the full headline and click on a headline to open an article in a new window with keywords highlighted. There is also a wide range of clip-sort-view options. The e-mail alert itself was excellent too, as it contained full bibliographic information as well as a short abstract of the item where the targeted keywords were located (users can specify whether to show the excerpt where the initial mention of the keywords appear, or where in the item the words are most highly concentrated).

Note that eWatch also has several other related services: NewsGroups monitors 66,000 Usenet groups and 16,000 Internet mailing lists; Online Services monitors specific consumer groups on AOL and CompuServe; Investor Message Boards monitors online investment discussion groups.

Bottom Line: All in all, we were very impressed with the coverage, features, and overall quality of eWatch and feel it is the best of the Web-based monitoring services.

WebClipping.com

www.webclipping.com
Los Angeles, CA
Founded in 1998 as a division of AllResearch Inc.

As we noted at the beginning of this report, we were unable to arrange for an actual trial of WebClipping, so we did not have the opportunity to provide a full evaluation. However, WebClipping did provide some feature and product data, so we do include it in our comparison chart.

Note that WebClipping focuses on assisting public relations agencies and others who specifically want to monitor mentions of their firm and products on Web pages, online news sites, and Usenet discussion groups.

YellowBrix

www.yellowbrix.com
Alexandria, VA
Founded by InfoSeek; launched as YellowBrix in 2000. In February 2004 YellowBrix merged with FluentMedia, a division of Tribune Media Services.

Target Market: Business and financial executives; Web site operators who need syndicated content.

Key Claims: Automated topic classification system; real-time alerts with replacements of older news versions with new updated versions.

Special Features: Over 1,000 preselected subject categories; can host service if required.

Test Results: A preliminary test established by the vendor determined that Yellow-Brix was unable to find any items for Alert #1 or #2, so these were not included. For Alert #3, only a few items were retrieved and all were relevant.

Sample Sources: The only source provider we received were articles from the AP Wire.

Intuitiveness and Ease of Set Up: Not applicable, as the alert was created by a vendor.

Comments: We liked the e-mail alerts, as the formatting was extremely clear with a hotlink, a big bold headline, the source's name, the first few lines from the article, the date and time of the news item, and our keywords highlighted in yellow. We then just clicked the item link to go to the full story (though, for some reason, the link stopped working after a day or so).

Bottom Line: We're not quite sure what to make of YellowBrix, since the vendor told us it would not be able to find anything on our initial two searches, and we only received a few AP stories on the broader one. Based on this performance, it would not be one of our top selections.

When scanning the charts, compare these important factors:

Coverage: In general, the more sources the better. Look also at the data for international coverage.

Type of Sources: The most common sources are digital newspapers and newswires. Some vendors also include electronic versions of print papers and trade journals, and some include online discussion groups and blogs.

Information Providers: In this category, we have listed the most sought after and premium business information providers. Only a few alert services include one or more of these suppliers.

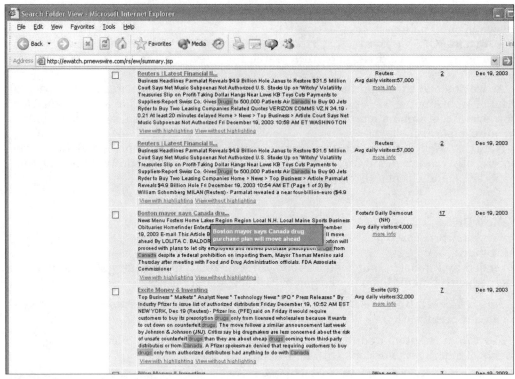

YellowBrix

User Controls: To avoid news alert overload, it is very important to be able to limit one's keywords to a source's title/headline, and, if possible, by individual source and/or geographic region.

Delivery: Virtually all alert services can provide the alert by either e-mail or on a Web site. A few offer extra features like wireless delivery or XML. Most allow the users to choose to obtain their alerts either on a continuous basis or on a predetermined time, such as once or twice a day. Another difference is in what you receive—while most provide a headline and abstract, some services only provide a headline.

Intranet Use: Do you want to integrate an alert service onto your intranet? Some vendors not only allow this, but also offer various administrative controls. Some will even let the client integrate its own internal news and announcements with the alert service.

Archive: The availability and length of an alert service's archive can vary quite a bit, as well as whether the archive is even searchable.

Special Features: A few alert services offer extras such as images or some level of data analysis or manipulation.

Pricing: A wide range of pricing schemes is made available from alert firms.

Customer Support: Easily available and quality telephone customer support is important for alert service users. Some offer such support 24 hours per day, 7 days a week, but most have more limited hours.

Here are explanations for the abbreviations and protocols used in the chart that follows:

Type Sources: A count for each type of source was provided where the vendor was able to supply the data. Sources that the vendor informed us were emphasized are highlighted in bold text.

User Controls: Limit alerts by: Headlines (H); Source Titles (S); Geographic Region (R).

Delivery / Frequency: D=Daily; 2/D=Twice per day; 3/D=Three times per day; W=Weekly; M=Monthly; Immed.=Immediately/Continuously.

Feature Comparison: Fee-Based/Premium News Alert Services						
	Burrelle's/ Luce NewsAlert	**CustomScoop**	**CyberAlert**	**Dialog NewsEdge**	**FNS NewsClips Online**	**FT.com Global Media Monitor**
Coverage						
--No. Sources	68K+	6,000+	13,000+	2,057	6,000+	Several hundred
--International	308 Canada; 568 other non-U.S.+ intl. print pubs.	1,500; 107 countries, 18 languages (original language)	30% and in 17 languages (original language)	YES	25%+	YES: global sources included
--Restricted to Web Sources	NO	YES	NO	NO	NO	NO
Type Sources						
--Newswires	YES (11)	**YES**	YES	YES	Online: 20	YES
--Print Papers	1,129	NO	NO	YES	NO	YES
--Online Papers	2,420	**YES**	YES	NO	**YES: 3,834**	YES
--Journals	2,679 (1,359*)	ONLINE	ONLINE	YES	ONLINE: 542	YES
--Usenet	YES (55K+)	NO	65,000+**	NO	NO	NO
--Listservs	NO	NO	NO	NO	NO	NO
--Blogs	NO	NO	SOME	NO	NO	NO
--Co. Directories	NO	NO	NO	YES	NO	NO
--Mkt. Res. Reports	NO	NO	NO	NO	NO	NO
--Invest. Reports	NO	NO	SOME	YES	NO	NO
--Other	TV and radio news broadcasts**	N.A.	TV networks and local stations	N.A.	TV and radio Web sites	NO
Providers Include						
--DJ/Factiva	NO	NO	NO	YES	NO	NO
--ProQuest	YES	NO	NO	YES	NO	NO
--Gale	NO	NO	NO	YES	NO	NO
--Hoover's	YES	NO	NO	YES	YES	NO
--Knight Ridder	YES	NO	NO	YES	NO	NO
--RDS	NO	NO	NO	NO	NO	NO
--Other	YES	N.A.	N.A.	N.A.	Bloomberg, Forbes.com, Financial Times, CBS MarketWatch	NO

	Burrelle's/ Luce NewsAlert	CustomScoop	CyberAlert	Dialog NewsEdge	FNS NewsClips Online	FT.com Global Media Monitor
User Controls -- No. of Alerts Allowed --Limit Alerts by --Boolean Searches	SEE BELOW	Unlimited H, R YES	Unlimited T, R YES including NEAR/ Proximity	150/user H, T, R YES including Boolean/ Proximity	Unlimited T, R YES	"Numerous" T, R YES
--On-the-Fly Searching Permitted	NO	YES, via InstantScoop	NO	YES	YES	YES
Delivery/ Frequency --Method	E-mail, Web	E-mail, Web, XML	E-mail, Web, XML to client's site	E-mail, Web, Scrolling (in Q1 2004)	E-mail, Web	E-mail, Wireless
--Frequency	Every two hours, or as needed upon request	D, 2D, Immed.	D	Immed.	D, 2/D	Immed.
--Real Time	NO (Crisis Alerts are available upon request)	NO	"Soon"	YES	NO	NO (though the service includes breaking news sources)
Intranet Use --Available --Admin. Controls --Ability to Integrate Firm's own Internal News	YES YES YES	Via XML feed NO YES	YES YES YES	YES YES YES	YES NO NO	NO NO NO
Archive --Available	YES	YES	YES	YES	NO	YES
--Backfile --Searchable	30 days YES, based upon a client's searching capabilities	60 days YES	Unlimited YES	90 days [1] YES	N.A. N.A.	Two years YES
Special Features --Images --Analysis	YES Upon request	NO NO	NO NO	NO NO	NO NO	NO NO

	Burrelle's/ Luce NewsAlert	CustomScoop	CyberAlert	Dialog NewsEdge	FNS NewsClips Online	FT.com Global Media Monitor
--Other	Upon request	Charting and graphing; monthly spreadsheet report; drill-down analysis *	N.A.	Shared Modules [2]	N.A.	N.A.
Pricing --Subscription Fee	$185/mo.	$299– $699/mo.	$125/mo.*** $195/mo.**** $295/mo.*****	Per seat, begins at $18,000/yr. for five users; optional for publishing, intranet redistribution, internal content processing	None	Upon request
--Other Fees	$3.88 per print clip/$10 per broadcast segment	NONE	NONE		Monthly flat rate w/one year contracts	N.A.
Customer Service --Phone Support --Hours/Times	YES 8 A.M.–6 P.M. EST (M–F)	YES 8 A.M.–8 P.M. EST (M–F)	YES 8 A.M.–6 P.M. EST (M–F + special evening/ weekend contacts)	YES 7 A.M.–7 P.M. EST (24/7 for urgent issues)	YES 9 A.M.–6 P.M. EST (M–F)	YES 8 A.M.–6 P.M. U.K. time

    * Drilling down is a feature whereby users can narrow and focus their search by "drilling down" into the listing of their news stories by keyword, then by state, and then by source.
    ** And 20,000+ Web-based message boards and forums.
    ***Per search string for regional monitoring.
    ****Per search string for national monitoring.
    *****Per search string for worldwide monitoring.
    (CyberAlert offers a 14-day free trial)

Dialog: NewsEdge

1. Variable—Base product provides 90 days and a utility to search select Dialog databases with an archive of up to 30 years. (Access to the NewsRoom database can be purchased providing a 2-year archive of 7,000+ publications.)
2. Shared Modules—The Shared Modules feature allows users within an organization to leverage the knowledge and experience of their colleagues. Users can create saved searches or collections of important links to internal or external resources. These Modules can be denoted as "shared" resources allowing all other users to access the information provided.

Burrelle's/Luce NewsAlert

- There are 1,359 "non-pubs" defined as publications that are indigenous only to the Web. This includes foreign publications that are only available via the Web, broadcast sites that are only available via the Web, and e-zines which are publications that are not available in print form at all, but are strictly electronic publications.

- NewsAlert also provides access to broadcast sources. It monitors most televised news broadcast stations in all of the top 100 markets and provides closed-captioned segments from all of these markets and monitored news segments from the top 50 markets. Radio news broadcast includes coverage of the top 100 markets during "Drive Time" (6 A.M.–9 A.M. and 3 P.M.–7 P.M.)
- Other providers include Gannett, USA Today, ABB, Newhouse Publishing, Thomson Publishing, NYT Newswire, LexisNexis.

User Controls: Burrelle's/Luce NewsAlert reports that its client service representatives will assist the user in coming up with search terms and, furthermore, reviews the alerts before sending them along to the client. According to a company representative, its editors typically discard 80 percent of the news that is electronically retrieved and sends the remaining 20 percent on to their clients which represent the news stories that match the *intent* of their search, not just their search terms.

Feature Comparison: Fee-Based/Premium News Alert Services

	Hoover's News Alerts	Moreover ci alerts	NewsNow Media Monitoring Service	PR Newswire eWatch	WebClipping.com	YellowBrix
Coverage						
--No. Sources	Approx. 600	6,000+	13,586	7,500	92,000+Web	3,000
--International	Approx. 20%	400 in a non-English language	U.K.: 40% Other: 60% English Language: 93%	Approx. 1,000 online		10%
--Restricted to Web Sources	NO	YES	YES	NO	YES	NO
Type Sources						
--Newswires	**YES**	YES: 15	YES	**YES**	YES: 99	**YES**
--Print Papers	**YES**	NO	NO	NO	YES: 2,700 pub.	**YES**
--Online Papers	YES	YES: 2,161	YES	YES	YES	**YES**
--Journals	**YES**	**ONLINE: 1,620**	ONLINE	YES	N.A.	**YES**
--Usenet	NO	**YES: 90**	NO	YES	YES	NO
--Listservs	NO	On request	NO	**YES**	NO	NO
--Blogs	NO	**YES: 65K+**	NO	NO	N.A.	NO
--Co. Directories	NO	SOME	NO	NO	NO	**YES**
				NO	NO	NO
--Mkt. Res. Reports	YES	**Online only**	NO			
--Invest. Reports	YES	**Online only**	NO	NO	NO	NO
--Other	N.A.	N.A.	Will add online news sources on request	Investor message boards; company Web sites on demand	NO	Co. financials, market data, audio, video, Internet radio, **photos**

	Hoover's News Alerts	Moreover ci alerts	NewsNow Media Monitoring Service	PR Newswire eWatch	WebClipping.com	YellowBrix
Providers Include						
--DJ/Factiva	SOME	NO	YES	NO	NO	NO
--ProQuest	NO	NO	NO	NO	NO	NO
--Gale	NO	NO	NO	NO	NO	NO
--Hoover's	YES	NO	NO	NO	NO	NO
--Knight Ridder	YES	NO	NO	NO	NO	NO
--RDS	NO	NO	NO	NO	NO	NO
--Other	AP, CMP, CNET, REED	N.A.	N.A.	N.A.	N.A.	N.A.
User Controls						
--No. of Alerts Allowed	Unlimited	Unlimited	Unlimited	Three per day	Unlimited	Five
--Limit Alerts by	N.A.	H, T, R	H, T, R	N.A.	N.A.	H, T, R & "context" **
--Boolean Searches	YES, incl. NEAR/ Proximity	YES, incl. NEAR/ Proximity	YES, but by NewsNow's own staff	YES, but performed by own staff	YES, no proximity	YES, including NEAR/Proximity
--On-the-Fly Searching Permitted	YES	YES	YES, but with restrictions	NO	NO	YES
Delivery/ Frequency						
--Method	E-mail	E-mail, Web	E-mail, Web	E-mail, Web	Customer database	E-mail, Web, Scrolling, Wireless, Web Services, Portlets Web Site plug-ins***
--Frequency	D, 2/D, Immed.	D, Immed.	*	3/D	D	Immed.
--Real Time	YES	YES	NO	NO	YES	YES
Intranet Use						
--Available	NO	YES	YES	NO	NO	YES
--Admin. Controls	YES	YES	NO	NO	N.A.	YES
--Ability to Integrate Firm's Own Internal News	NO	On request	NO	NO	N.A.	YES
Archive						
--Available	YES	YES	YES	YES	YES	YES
--Backfile	30 days	Varies by source	30 days	Six months	Six months	30 days
--Searchable	YES	Varies by source	Limited	NO	NO	YES

	Hoover's News Alerts	Moreover ci alerts	NewsNow Media Monitoring Service	PR Newswire eWatch	WebClipping.com	YellowBrix
Special Features --Images --Analysis	NO NO	NO NO, but assign Sources with a quality indicator	NO NO	NO NO, but filtering for Usenet groups	NO For extra fee	YES NO
--Other	N.A.	N.A.	N.A.	Content translation	N.A.	N.A.
Pricing --Subscription Fee	$2,000/yr.+	Per user license $5,000+	Monthly; average ranges from £175 – £300/mo.	$3,900/yr. for five users	$500/mo. OR $1,300/yr.	Monthly based on no. of subject areas per company or site
--Other Fees	NONE	NONE	NONE	NONE	NONE	NONE
Customer Service --Phone Support --Hours/Times	YES 8 A.M.–6 P.M. CST M–F	YES 9 A.M.–6 P.M. GMT and 24/7 emergency	YES 9:00–18:00 GMT (M–F)	YES 8 A.M.–8 P.M. EST (M–F; weekends by pager)	YES 9 A.M.–5 P.M. PST	YES 24/7

*Web: updated every 5 to 7 minutes; e-mail frequency: available once per day to once per hour.

** Context is determined by a proprietary software program called ArchiText.

*** YellowBrix focuses on syndication. Its methods of delivery are via either private-labeled hosted Web sites for companies; interactive XML API for download via HTTP, to format on the fly with style sheets (XSL); or by Web services/universal portlets where YellowBrix hosts plug-n-play Web services that are integrated onto corporate portals and intranets.

Nexcerpt: An Intriguing Premium News Service for Info Pros

The article below is excerpted from the March 2004 issue of *The Information Advisor.*

We recently came across a very intriguing news alert service called Nexcerpt (www.nexcerpt.com) that operates quite a bit differently than the ones we recently reviewed in our two-part series on alert services. While not perfect, and a little pricey compared to others, we feel that its unique features and its intelligent design make it an ideal niche product for information professionals. It would be particularly appealing if you manage a centralized information center and want to increase your visibility and value to the rest of your organization.

Background

Nexcerpt, which is based in Kalamazoo, Mich. and employs eight people, was launched in early 2003 by husband and wife team Gary and Julie Stock. The Stocks had previously been associated with an Internet monitoring company called InGenius Technologies.

Nexcerpt scans about 4,700 Web-based news sources, retrieving about 40,000 articles daily. Like other alert services, users create a specific keyword profile and receive a daily e-mail with an abstract and a URL to the relevant articles. Nexcerpt offers several unusual features and capabilities for a Web-based alert service. Among them:

- **Publishing:** Incoming alerts can be published to a Web site or intranet, allowing the administrator to easily produce an online news service.
- **Audience Designation:** The administrator can determine which groups of people in the organization should receive which news alerts.
- **Draft/Annotation Capabilities:** The administrator has the ability to review a draft of the alerts before they are officially published, add commentary, and even append additional news excerpts not picked up by Nexcerpt.

Our Trial

We signed up for a 14-day free trial to evaluate the service. The interface for creating our keyword alerts was pretty simple. We simply gave a name to our various profiles and clicked the fill-in boxes to input our keyword statement, using the AND, OR, and NOT operators.

Clicking on "help" provided excellent, context-sensitive search assistance. Nexcerpt searches for all word variations automatically, unless a word is placed in quotation marks (quotation marks should also be used for phrases). Clicking on the "expert" mode link didn't really offer any additional search options but did provide the opportunity to string a longer number of Boolean search statements together and use parentheses. We looked to see if there was an option to limit our search to words that occurred only in the title or headline or use other field limitations, but did not see any.

Until this point, Nexcerpt operated like most alert services. However, we noted a couple of special options. One was the ability to fine tune our search based on a "theme." Nexcerpt groups its sources into 33 subject themes, ranging from alternative, arts and culture, and business to government, industries, and world news. Interestingly, Nexcerpt makes a conscious decision to exclude sports news because, Julie Stock explained, sports news makes up a very high percentage of news on the Web and is unwanted noise for most of Nexcerpt's clients.

Clicking on the "resource selection" link let us view all titles or all titles within a theme, and select or deselect specific titles to include or exclude. We could also pull up titles to include or exclude based on their geographic location or by keyword. This is an excellent tool for focusing an alert just on items from favorite sources or eliminating those sources that are retrieving irrelevant hits.

By default, all themes are set to a "medium" relevancy retrieval. However, we could also set each title in a theme to a retrieval setting of never, low, medium, or high.

Another very useful option when setting up our keyword profiles was to designate a particular group ("audience") to receive a specific keyword alert. Since we were testing this on our own, we did not need to invoke it, but it would be an extremely useful option for organizational usage.

After inputting some settings on preferred time of e-mail delivery and a few other small details, we saved our alert and waited for our results.

Receiving a Draft

Each day, Nexcerpt sent us a "draft" of the day's alerts for us to review before it was officially "published" to the designated audience (in our trial, that was simply ourselves). We received several relevant hits from our keyword searches, and our keywords were highlighted in the excerpts. Stock told us that Nexcerpt's algorithm ranks news items based on a "resource authority" factor assigned to each news source, ranking each one based on criteria like the publication's circulation, and (as Google does to determine its rankings) what other sites are linking in to the source. Our only problem was that we received a few irrelevant hits on a one-word search due to Nexcerpt's automatic stemming—this was fixed by placing the word in quotation marks.

Here, we had the ability to:

- Add a prologue.
- Eliminate any unwanted news items.
- Make comments on each specific news item retrieved.
- Add additional relevant news excerpts of our own, along with a URL.
- Add an epilogue.

When we were satisfied with our review and the changes we made, we clicked "publish" and Nexcerpt sent out the completed day's alert.

One of the tricky things in working with any news alert service is fine tuning it to make sure that what is being retrieved is on target. Nexcerpt was impressive in what it offered here. Clicking on a link called "correlated keywords" identified other words that appeared most often in close proximity to our keywords. This helped us understand the context in which our keywords were appearing and provided suggestions for adding other keywords. Clicking a link labeled "query statistics" provided a graphical view of how each specific keyword "performed" during the last week in terms of number of items it retrieved. And we were most impressed when one of Nexcerpt's librarians in customer service sent us this unsolicited e-mail:

Robert:

Regarding your "low carb market" query: Because Nexcerpt is punctuation-sensitive, I have added "low-carb" and "low-carbohydrate" to your query so you capture both forms of the words.

Please let me know if I can be of further assistance.

Pricing

A subscription to Nexcerpt, which includes up to 10 different keyword queries and full publishing privileges, costs $200/month. That fee includes the right to send alerts to clients and others *outside* of one's own organization as well.

Overall Evaluation

We quickly became a very big fan of Nexcerpt. We think that the human intelligence that went into creating the product, the analytical tools, the annotation and publishing features, and its overall design make this a superb tool for business information professionals.

We appreciated how Nexcerpt's annotation capabilities can be used to customize incoming news into a larger context relevant to your organization, facilitate internal discussion and knowledge sharing, and ultimately increase your visibility and increase both the real and perceived value of the information center. Nexcerpt also integrates human intelligence into an automated procedure, offering the recipients of the alerts the best of both worlds.

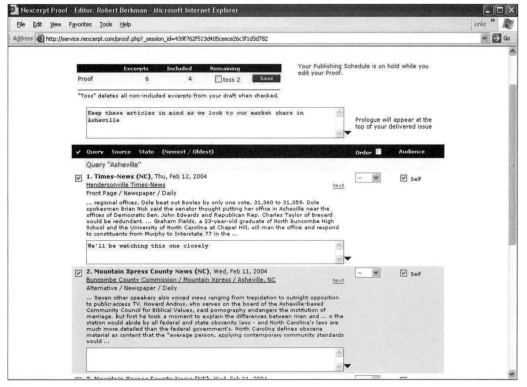

Nexcerpt

All that said, we should point out that Nexcerpt doesn't offer everything. For one, Nexcerpt's sources are limited to the Web, and if you rely on this service as your major provider of information, you (and your audience) will be missing news and information from critical non-Web sources such as articles published in print-based academic and trade journals and newspapers like *The Wall Street Journal*. Ideally, you'd supplement a subscription with Nexcerpt with access to a vendor like Factiva, where you could search electronic feeds of important print sources.

And you need to check that Nexcerpt is including Web sources most important to you. One of our keyword searches was to track mentions of "Asheville," a small city in North Carolina. We were surprised to discover that Nexcerpt only included two relatively obscure media sources for Asheville, but not the region's major newspaper, the *Asheville Citizen Times*, which is on the Web. Fortunately, users can suggest sources they think should be covered on Nexcerpt, and, says Stock, the firm is likely to oblige and add it, either as a special source just for that user, or as a wider source available to all its clients.

Also, while we liked the search interface, we would have appreciated having the ability to limit our keywords to an article's headline or title, which is an important tool when doing broad searches to avoid getting too many hits.

Chapter 6

Traditional Online Vendors' News Alert Services

The final broad cut of news alert services suitable for serious news monitoring and research are those we call "traditional online vendors." Here we are referring to those few premium online database vendors that have a long-time presence in the information industry as a preferred source for professional online searching. These firms also offer their subscribers e-mail alert tools for staying up-to-date on the news and keeping up with the latest information sources as they are added to the service.

This group of vendors differs from those listed in the previous three categories in a few significant ways:

1. The primary focus of these firms is not just to offer a news alert service, but to be a full-service, substantive online database vendor. The alerting service is made available as a convenient, useful feature to its subscribers.
2. Because these vendors gather information from publishers of all kinds, and not just Web-based news sites, subscribers are more likely to get alerts to non-Web news and information sources, such as articles published in the trade and academic press. In some cases, subscribers can even be alerted to other broader types of news sources too, such as the latest market research reports.
3. Because the traditional customers for these services have been librarians, information professionals, and other expert searchers, this group of vendors tends to offer the most sophisticated search features and options.

Here are the information providers that fall in this category:

- Dialog: NewsRoom
- Factiva: Track Module
- Intelligence Data: InSite 2
- LexisNexis: Personal News

Profiles and Test Results

Dialog NewsRoom
www.dialognewsroom.com
Cary, NC
NewsRoom was launched by Dialog in 2002.

Target Market: Business/financial analysts; sales and marketing professionals; market researchers; engineering/science/technology researchers; information professionals and librarians.

Key Claims: Extensive non-Web news collection.

Dialog NewsRoom

Special Features: InfoSort Indexing: market sector, scope. Deep searchable archive.

Test Results: Nothing retrieved on the first two searches, though an archive search retrieved earlier items on the Alert #2 search. On the Alert #3, we received several items daily, and nearly all were relevant.

Sample Sources: *AP, Pittsburgh Post Gazette, Canadian Press, Providence Journal Bulletin.*

Intuitiveness and Ease of Set Up: Not as simple as some others, as the alert creation requires knowledge of the appropriate protocols and use of tags (which NewsRoom imported from Profound's NewsLine service, which itself has been subsumed under NewsRoom). In March 2004, Dialog enhanced and updated its subject terminology and renamed these "SmartTerms." However, the help screen is very good and it is extremely valuable to learn how to use these precision tags. One quirk is that to effectively use Boolean operators, you need to remember to use specified symbols and not the standard Boolean text.

Comments: NewsRoom offers a great deal of precision search power. The e-mail alerts provide a list of headlines, sources, dates, and word counts. Users can then download the listing or go to a URL to view the full stories, where the articles are nicely reformatted.

Bottom Line: An excellent choice for conducting very precise searches and getting access to a deep archive. Remember, though, that NewsRoom does not search the open Web, so you may obtain fewer results on certain obscure searches that would have retrieved more items from Internet-based newspapers and niche Web sites.

Factiva: Track Module
www.factiva.com/integration/factivamodules/track.asp?node=menuElem1496
Princeton, NJ

Factiva was founded 1999 as a joint venture between Dow Jones and Reuters.

Target Market: Business executives; salespeople; and marketing professionals.

Key Claims: 120 newswires; 8,000 business-oriented premium sources including *The Wall Street Journal*; sources in 22 languages.

Special Features: Historical market data; company reports; optimized for intranet use, administrative controls.

Test Results: Nothing retrieved on the first two searches; for Alert #3, a small number of highly relevant results were retrieved.

Sample Sources: *Pharma MarketLetter, Associated Press, NPR, The Globe and Mail, AP, Time, Market News Publishing.*

Intuitiveness and Ease of Set Up: Simple and intuitive set up.

Comments: Although the set up is simple, Factiva Track Module users can use numerous precision filters and search options, including the option to employ a variety of powerful proximity operators. The e-mailed results offer a nice bibliographic summary with a short abstract (though the URLs provided are extremely long). Clicking on a retrieved result links the user to a very cleanly reformatted page. Note that we needed to click on "exclude republished news" to eliminate duplicate items.

Bottom Line: Outstanding business sources that go beyond typical Web-based news sites and powerful search options make Factiva Track Module a true business professional's choice. Remember though, that Factiva does not include any Web-only sources.

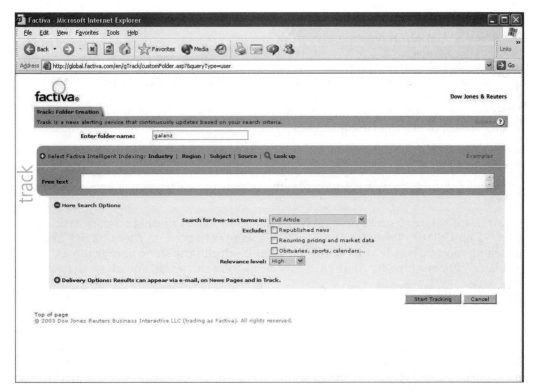

Factiva: Track Module

Intelligence Data: InSite 2
www.insite2.gale.com
Boston, MA
InSite 2 was created by the Gale Group, which is part of Thomson Corporations' Intelligence Data. Intelligence Data became part of Thomson's Dialog division in January 2002.

Target Market: Business researchers.

Key Claims: Premium content from leading industry trade journals.

Special Features: Deep archive; in-depth trade journal coverage and company profiles. Breaks results into three main categories: Industry Articles and Analyses, News and Key Events, Newsletters and Opinion.

Test Results: Nothing retrieved for first two alerts. On Alert #3, only a few items were retrieved, but all were relevant.

Sample Sources: *Time, Forbes, Pharma MarketLetter, British Medical Journal, Cardiovascular Week, Advertising Age.*

Intuitiveness and Ease of Set Up: InSite 2 was extremely easy to set up, with a very well designed interface.

Comments: InSite 2 focuses primarily on trade journals as opposed to breaking news sites. The service offers excellent power search features to ensure relevancy and provides a superb help screen. We particularly liked the ability to test a search and view results instantly and clearly. The e-mail alerts provided a clear bibliography, but no summary or abstract.

Bottom Line: Highly recommended for ongoing in-depth coverage of a topic, but not for tracking breaking news. InSite 2 also has one of the best searchable archives of the vendors we tested.

LexisNexis: Personal News
www.nexis.com/research
Miamisburg, OH
LexisNexis was founded 1973. LexisNexis is owned by Reed Elsevier plc.

Target Market: Librarians; information professionals; lawyers; news media; corporations; government agencies; academia.

Key Claims: Huge collection of full-text newspaper and general news sources. Extensive legal, business patent, trademark, scientific sources.

Special Features: Extremely wide breadth of types of searchable sources; extensive archive.

Test Results: LexisNexis' Personal News did quite well in finding obscure articles on Alert #1 on Galanz. Though no new articles were retrieved on Alert #2, its archive turned up recent items that included the word Lipitor in the same paragraph as "market share." For our broader Alert #3, many items were retrieved, and all were relevant.

Sample Sources: *EIU ViewsWire, Financial Times, USA Today, AP, Deseret News, Fortune, CNBC News Transcripts.*

Intuitiveness and Ease of Set Up: Excellent and very easy to set up.

Comments: As LexisNexis customers know, clients have many advanced search options available, including various proximity operator options. There is a checkbox for removing duplicates. We found the customer service to be outstanding. The e-mail alerts were very good in that they provided a full bibliography with our keywords in context.

Intelligence Data: InSite 2

Bottom Line: There are two reasons why you might choose LexisNexis as your alert service. One is the ability to be extraordinarily precise in creating your search. The other is the wide range of professional content that can be searched. For example, you can specify a search in a set of deep sources categorized as general news, company news, industry news, people news, world news, company information, government information, medical information, country information, public records, legal information, and markets. If you need to regularly search and track a very specific type of business, legal, or regulatory issue covered in specialized professional publications, we'd advise the LexisNexis service. Keep in mind, though, that you do need to be an existing client of LexisNexis in order to use its alert service.

When scanning the chart, compare these important factors:

Coverage: In general, the more sources the better. Look also at the data for international coverage.

Type of Sources: The most common sources are digital newspapers and newswires. Some vendors also include electronic versions of print papers and trade journals, and some include online discussion groups and blogs.

Information Providers: In this category, we have listed the most sought after and premium business information providers. Only a few alert services include one or more of these suppliers.

User Controls: To avoid news alert overload, it is very important to be able to limit one's keywords to a source's title/headline and, if possible, by individual source and/or geographic region.

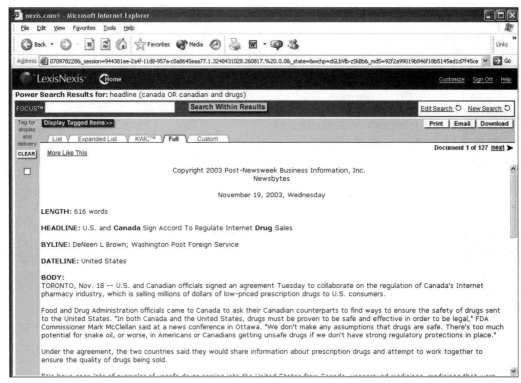

LexisNexis: Personal News

Delivery: Virtually all alert services can provide the alert either by e-mail or on a Web site. A few offer extra features like wireless delivery or XML. Most allow the users to choose to obtain their alerts either on a continuous basis or on a predetermined time, such as once or twice a day. Another difference is in what you receive—while most provide a headline and abstract, some services only provide a headline.

Intranet Use: Do you want to integrate an alert service onto your intranet? Some vendors not only allow this, but also offer various administrative controls. Some will even let the client integrate its own internal news and announcements with the alert service.

Archive: The availability and length of an alert service's archive can vary quite a bit, as well as whether the archive is even searchable.

Special Features: A few alert services offer extras such as images or some level of data analysis or manipulation.

Pricing: A wide range of pricing schemes is made available from alert firms.

Customer Support: Easily available and quality telephone customer support is important for alert service users. Some offer such support 24 hours per day, 7 days a week, but most have more limited hours.

Here are explanations for the abbreviations and protocols used in the chart that follows:

Type Sources: A count for each type of source was provided where the vendor was able to supply the data. Sources that the vendor informed us were emphasized are highlighted in bold text.

User Controls: Limit alerts by: Headlines (H); Source Titles (S); Geographic Region (R).

Delivery / Frequency: D=Daily; 2/D=Twice per day; 3/D=Three times per day; W=Weekly; M=Monthly; Immed.=Immediately/Continuously.

Feature Comparison: Traditional Online Vendors' News Alert Services				
	Dialog NewsRoom	Factiva TrackModule	Intelligence Data InSite 2	LexisNexis Personal News
Coverage				
--No. Sources	Approx. 7,500	Approx. 8,000	Approx. 4,900 active	14,000
--International	42%, includes some translations of non-English sources	22 languages, 118 countries	YES	6,800 +
--Restricted to Web Sources	NO	NO	NO	NO
Type Sources				
--Newswires	YES: 191	YES: 300	YES	YES: 140
--Print Papers	YES: 1,070	YES: 1,000+	YES	YES: 1600 (print +online)
--Online Papers	YES	NO	NO	YES: 4,100+
--Journals	YES: 2,985	YES: 3,000+	**YES**	NO
--Usenet	NO	NO	NO	NO
--Listservs	NO	NO	NO	NO
--Blogs	NO	NO	NO	NO
--Co. Directories	YES: 3	30K company reports	YES	YES: 140+
--Mkt. Res. Reports	NO	Coming Soon	NO	YES: 150+

	Dialog NewsRoom	Factiva TrackModule	Intelligence Data InSite 2	LexisNexis Personal News
--Invest. Reports	NO	NO	YES	YES
--Other	YES: See below*	N.A.	N.A.	YES: 700+ Many types of other sources**
Providers Include				
--DJ/Factiva	NO	YES	NO	NO
--ProQuest	YES	YES	NO	NO
--Gale	YES	YES	YES	YES
--Hoover's	NO	YES	NO	YES
--Knight Ridder	YES	YES	NO	YES
--RDS	YES	NO	NO	YES
--Other	Global Reporter	Reuters	NO	Over 60 **
User Controls				
--No. of Alerts Allowed	Unlimited	25 Folders	Unlimited	Unlimited
--Limit Alerts by	H, T, R	H, T, R	H, T, R	H, T, R
--Boolean Searches	YES, including NEAR/ Proximity	YES, including NEAR, ADJn	YES, including NEAR/ Proximity	YES, including Proximity
--On-the-Fly Searching Permitted	YES	YES	YES	YES
Delivery/ Frequency				
--Method	E-mail, Web	E-mail, Web	E-mail, Web	E-mail, Web
--Frequency	D, W, M	D, 2/D, Immed.	D, W	D, 2/D, 3/D, W
--Real Time	NO	NO (but available w/Factiva Alerts)	NO	Via 3rd party: PINNACOR on nexis.com

	Dialog NewsRoom	Factiva TrackModule	Intelligence Data InSite 2	LexisNexis Personal News
Intranet Use				
--Available	NO	YES	NO	Via Nexis.com shared news
--Admin. Controls	NO	YES	NO	YES
--Ability to Integrate Firm's own Internal News	NO	Via Editor or Publisher product	NO	NO (need LexisNexis Publisher)
Archive				
--Available	YES	YES	YES	YES
--Backfile	Indefinitely	Varies by pub.	Five year rolling	90 days
--Searchable	YES	YES	YES	YES
Special Features				
--Images	NO	YES: KRphoto	NO	YES
--Analysis	NO	Upcoming via integration with IBM's WebFountain	NO	NO
--Other	InfoSort indexing for market sectors, scope, companies, geographic region	N.A.	N.A.	N.A.

	Dialog NewsRoom	Factiva TrackModule	Intelligence Data InSite 2	LexisNexis Personal News
Pricing --Subscription Fee	Available or transactional (see below)	$69/yr.	Monthly fee based on full-text document usage	Subscription rates vary by type of customer and contract
--Other Fees	Transactional : $2.95 per document	$2.95/article + various corporate and enterprise pricing	NONE	N.A.
Customer Service --Phone Support --Hours/Times	YES 24/M–F	YES 24/7	YES 8 A.M.–6 P.M. M–F EST (5 P.M. Fridays)	YES 24/7

Dialog NewsRoom
* Newsletters: 676
Academic Journals: 1,486
Broadcast Sources: 50
Magazines: 818
Press Releases: 22
Reports: 13
Miscellaneous: 118

LexisNexis Personal News
** Other sources included with count:
Biographical: 20+
State Legislative: 100+
Federal Legislative: 5
Regulatory: 1
Reference: 200+
Intellectual Property: 10 authorities and 1,000+ various materials

** Other major business information providers include: A.M. Best, Bloomberg, Claritas, Company Intelligence, Creditreform, D&B, Disclosure, EIU, Espicom, Experian, Extel, Financial Post Corporate Surveys, Hoppenstedt ABC, Integra, Latin American Company Database, Major Companies Database, Market Guide, Marketshare Reporter, Mergerstat, Nelson's Nikkei, OneSource CorpTech, Roper/Harris/Starch, Standard & Poor's Thomson Bank Directories, Worldscope, and Zacks.

Chapter 7

Other Specialized
News Alert Services

This report has focused specifically on the most comprehensive and broadest news alert services—that is, those that deliver general and business news stories culled from many hundreds or thousands of different news sources, covering virtually any topic.

However, there are also scores, perhaps hundreds, of very *specialized* e-mail-based news alert services. These do not scan hundreds or thousands of general news sources but instead focus on monitoring a particular niche. Business-focused niche alert services would include, for instance, new patent filings, recent mergers, company filings, and so forth.

To give you a flavor of some of these useful—and largely free—alerting services, we have pulled together the names and URLs of several of the most interesting ones.

New Patent Filings: Patent Alert
www.patentalert.com/
Patent Alert will e-mail, at no charge, notifications of new patent filings. Users can choose to be alerted to just those patents filed under one of dozens of predefined topical categories created by Patent Alert, or they may create a custom keyword search. Users can also choose to get alerts on a weekly, biweekly, or monthly basis.

New Sec Filings: SEC Info
www.secinfo.com/$/SignUp.asp
SEC Info sends e-mail alerts on new filings from U.S. companies to the SEC's EDGAR and to Canada's equivalent SEDAR electronic filing systems.

New Mergers, Acquisitions, and Deals: The Daily Deal Alerts
thedeal.ewhsp.com/cgi/subscribe.html
If you sign up with The Daily Deal Alerts, you'll be informed of the latest business deals, including mergers and acquisitions, bankruptcies, company sales, and so on, that are tracked by The Deal.com Web site.

Company Events: PrecisionAlert
www.precisionalert.com/PrecisionAlertEntry.asp
PrecisionAlert will alert you, via e-mail, to any upcoming investor relations' events, such as conference calls that are held by whatever companies you specify.

Company Conference Calls: CallStreet Reports
www.callstreet.com
Users can receive e-mail alerts that provide access to transcripts of quarterly conference calls and earnings calls held by public companies.

Canadian News: FPinfomart.ca
www.fpinfomart.ca/prod/prod_start.php
FPinfomart, a product of the *Financial Post*, specializes in monitoring media sources in Canada. Users can obtain e-mail alerts to new stories that match their keyword profile.

Note that another service that monitors Canadian news, but focuses on French-language media, is available by a firm called Newscan.com (www.newscan.com).

Note that both of these services are fully-featured, fee-based subscription services that also offer a full range of searchable online databases.

Just-Published Market Research Reports: MarketResearch.com
digbig.com/3tcr
The market research report aggregator MarketResearch.com will send an e-mail every two weeks to alert you to any new market research reports it has entered into its database, for whatever industry categories you specify.

New Industry News: SmartBrief
www.smartbrief.com/signup/
On this site, you can sign up to get a free "Daily Brief" that aggregates news from various Web-based news services on several industries: associations and professional societies; aviation; biotech, medical device, drug, and food regulatory; cable and broadband; capital markets; confectionery; construction; education (K-12); financial service; food, beverage, and consumer packaged goods; franchising; and grocery/retail.

New Security Litigation: Securities Litigation Watch
slw.issproxy.com/
This site tracks thousands of securities class actions going back over a decade and will alert subscribers whenever a new case is filed or settled.

New Domain Name Dispute Decisions: WIPO Domain Name Dispute Resolution Service
arbiter.wipo.int/subscribe/decisions.html
Signing up with this alert service keeps you up-to-date on the latest domain name decisions taken by WIPO panels.

White Papers: KnowledgeAlert
ka.bitpipe.com
Sign up to be notified when white papers are published on a subject category you select. Bitpipe makes other IT research-related alerts available as well.

Health-Related News: U.K. Health News
www.bmj.com/uknews
Here you can sign up to receive daily e-mail summaries of health-related stories appearing in U.K. national newspapers.

Local and Regional News: Topix.net
www.topix.net
This is a fascinating news aggregation site that lets users zero in on Web-based news stories by a local geographic region. Although no alerting mechanism was available when we tried out Topix.net, we have been informed that one is expected to be introduced in the near future.

Company Press Releases: Businesswire.com
www.businesswire.com
If you want to be alerted to company press releases, you can sign up for e-mail alerts at Businesswire. Businesswire has said that "communications' professionals," which include librarians, may register to receive free e-mail headlines, customizable by various areas such as ticker, subject, geographic region, or keyword. The general public may also sign up for selected news releases from specified companies that offer the service through Businesswire by going to the site's "company news archives."

Broadcast Video Clips: ShadowTV
www.shadowtv.com
This innovative—but premium-priced—site will send an e-mail to a subscriber when his or her keywords are spoken on selected news, public affairs, and other broadcasts like CNBC or CNN. That e-mail will contain a link, and by clicking the link, the subscriber can actually view a video clip of that broadcast segment that contained the keywords right on the desktop. (For more on ShadowTV, see the review in the October 2003 issue of *The Information Advisor*, Vol. 15, No. 10, p. 1.)

Again, these are just a few examples of specialized e-mail alert services. If there's a particular subject that you'd like to monitor via an e-mail alert, but you don't know if any such alert is available, you might try doing a basic search on the Web to see what turns up. For example, say you wanted to find out if there were any alerts that were related to the publishing industry. You could just go to a search engine, like Google, and input the keyword statement

"publishing industry" "e-mail alerts" OR "news alerts"

and then review your results.

Reputation Management Monitoring

Note too that another type of specialized news alert service would include firms like Biz360 and Converseon. These firms offer services that may work similarly to a general news alert service in that sites, news, and talk are monitored and aggregated, but their focus is specifically on helping firms with a discipline called "Reputation Management." Here the vendor works closely with the firm in actively tracking and even influencing how the companies and their products are discussed over the Internet.

As we were going to press, Factiva was getting ready to introduce a reputation management tool built on IBM's WebFountain "data mining" software, which was created as a tool for "intelligently" mining the Web to look for trends, relations, and patterns and creating sense from the mountains of data and information on the Web (www.almaden.ibm.com/webfountain/). Factiva's WebFountain is being promoted as a way companies can obtain insights as to the reputation on the Net. For more information on WebFountain, link to www.factiva.com/webfountain/.

Individual News Site Alerts

In addition to specialized subject-oriented alerts, there are countless *individual* online newspapers and news/informational sites that offer an e-mail alert service to its own readers who want to keep up with the latest news from that source. Here is a handful of news and information sites that we've come across that offer this alerting service:

CNET: News.com
news.com.com/2030-52-5149595.html
Subscribers can receive e-mail alerts on technology-oriented news.

The Atlanta Journal-Constitution
www.ajc.com/
    Users can obtain headlines, mid-day alerts, and other news and informational features from this Web version of a leading daily newspaper.

Guardian Unlimited
www.guardian.co.uk
The Guardian is a very well known left-of-center British daily newspaper.

Harvard Business Online
www.hbsp.harvard.edu
These e-mail alerts provide news and summaries of new works available from Harvard Business School Publishing.

Jane's Defence Weekly: E-mail Alert
www2.janes.com/public/alerts.html
Users can sign up with Jane's alerts to keep up with news from this leading defense industry information provider.

StartUpJournal.com
www.startupjournal.com/e-mailcenter/
StartUpJournal.com, a product of *The Wall Street Journal*, offers e-mail alerts on its articles and updates on issues of interest to entrepreneurs and small businesses.

India on Mobile
nri.indiatimes.com/indiatimes/nri/intro.jsp
The Times of India is an English-language online newspaper that covers news about India and offers a wireless e-mail alert service.

The Next Big Thing? Wireless Alerts

    While not quite ready for prime time, several sites and services have been introducing *wireless* alerts, where users can obtain breaking news via a cell phone or other hand-held device. Given the growth of wireless communications, you can expect to see more of these as time goes on. There are still some issues though, that have not been fully resolved. The issues are both technical—related to standards and compatibility matters—as well as content-related, e.g., will a tiny screen be large enough to be practically useful? Do you really need alerts sent to your cell phone?

    Below are names of some vendors that offer wireless alerts. Note that these services do not permit users to input specific keywords to create custom alerts, though some allow users to limit their alerts to a selection of broad subject and industry categories.

ABC News
abcnews.go.com/sections/wireless/DailyNews/Wireless.html
This service offers breaking news and political updates on a smart cell phone for $1.99 per month.

AP Digital
www.apdigitalnews.com/headlines.html
Headlines are delivered by the AP to wireless devices. Users can choose subjects for delivery based on broad subject categories.

AvantGo

www.avantgo.com

AvantGo, part of iAnywhere, is owned by Sybase, and allows subscribers to browse from and select from hundreds of different "channels" to subscribe to text messaging news alerts on enhanced technology cell phones (a "smart phone") or handheld devices. A listing of business news-oriented channels can be found at my.avantgo.com/browse/851/. Some examples of general news and business-oriented news channels that can be downloaded and subscribed to via AvantGo include:

- BusinessWeek.com
- Fool.com Quotes and News
- Inc.com IPO's
- Hoover's IPO Update
- The Deal.com
- Silicon.com
- Industry Week
- New York Times—Technology
- New York Times—Business
- Fast Company
- LatinTrade.com
- ITWorld Canada
- Zacks Investment Research
- CNN
- CNET News
- Bloomberg
- PCWorld.com

CBS MarketWatch

cbs.marketwatch.com/mobile/default.asp?siteID=mktw

CBS MarketWatch will deliver company, market, and stock news to a hand-held device or mobile phone. See Chapter 3 for the review of the free CBS MarketWatch alert service.

Forbes.com Alerts

www.forbes.com/alerts/

Forbes offers a variety of general breaking business news alerts, including wireless text messaging delivery.

Money.net

www.money.net/products/products_alerts.php

Money.net offers streaming market data such as stock prices, high/low volume, and bid/ask alerts via wireless alerts.

PCQuote

www.pcquote.com/my/welcome.php

Like Money.net, PCQuote offers wireless stock and market data.

Yahoo! Mobile

mobile.yahoo.com/wireless/alert

The Yahoo! free alert service was covered in Chapter 3. In addition to offering that news alert service, Yahoo! also offers breaking news from Reuters and AP to users' mobile devices.

Chapter 8

Strategies for Getting the Most Out of a News Alert Service

After you've decided on a news alert vendor, you'll then want to make sure that you set up your profile and manage the service so that it best serves your needs and allows you to get the most value out of your news alert service.

Getting a Head Start

If you've selected a free news alert, you can spend a fair amount of time experimenting and playing with different searches to find out which searches work best for you, without worrying about costs. But what if you've chosen a fee-based service? In that case, you should check to see if you can arrange for a free trial. Several fee-based news alert services (such as HighBeam and Nexcerpt) offer this option. Not only does a trial allow you to discover if you really like the service enough to pay for it, but it also gives you a test period to try out your searches, see what kinds of results are being received, make any tweaks, and finalize what works best for you in matters like timing of delivery and the amount of information you want to receive in the alert.

Setting Up Your Profile

Once you've made a decision to sign up with an alert service, you need to create your profile. Typically, you'll do this by going to that alert service's Web site, finding the right page for inputting your keywords, and then choosing from various format and delivery options.

In order to create an effective alert, though, CyberAlert's president Bill Comcowich says that there is a preliminary step that you should take first. He advises new users to spend a little bit of time before constructing the keyword profile to think about overall objectives, and to develop a specification for the search that reflects those objectives. For example, Comcowich says that one might sign up with a news monitoring service to achieve any of these following objectives:

- Corporate reputation monitoring
- Brand monitoring
- Competitor monitoring
- Issues monitoring

Other reasons that one may want a news alert service could include:

- Keeping up with industry news
- Keeping up with news on emerging technologies
- Keeping up with news that impacts customers and client base
- Monitoring political and social developments in important regions in the world

Comcowich says that another matter to think about ahead of time is *who* is going to see the clips and how the clips will be utilized. So if you are in charge of setting up an alert service for staffers throughout your organization, you will probably first want to conduct a short information audit to get answers to that question. While the topic of how to create an information audit is beyond the scope of this report (though you can read an article on the topic in the September 1997 Knowledge Management Supplement of *The Information Advisor*), a good information audit of your staff on the introduction of a news alert service would inquire and find answers to questions like:

- What *kind* of breaking and timely news is most important for you to learn about and why?
- How are you currently obtaining that news, if at all?
- What are the *titles* of the most valuable news sources you are relying on now? Which are most critical to you? What do you like about those sources in particular?
- How are you *accessing* those sources now? Is the information coming to you in a timely and organized manner? Why or why not?
- What would a "perfect" news alert service look like to you?

These kinds of information are important to think about ahead of time so that when you are faced with options and alternatives in creating your news profile, you can make choices that are going to best serve your overall goals.

Setting Up Your Profile

Once you feel confident about which news alert service you wish to sign up with, and you feel that you have a good grasp on your overall objectives, it's time to actually begin creating the keywords that will track the news topics you want to monitor and make various decisions as to how you'd like your news alert service to operate.

As we've illustrated earlier in this report, each alert service has its own methods and options for creating an alert. But there are also some general principles and overall advice that we can offer here that would apply to virtually any alert service. Here's what to think about.

Determine the Best Keywords

Many of you who are reading this guide are experienced researchers and already know the art and skill of creating the most effective keywords for a database search or for use on an Internet search engine. But for those of you who may not be so experienced, let's go over just a few basic pointers. Following these short tips could make the difference between a news alert that works for you and one that is a failure:

- Make your keywords as specific as possible, e.g., a search on Lipitor is much better than a search on drugs or on pharmaceuticals.
- Use multiple word phrases where possible, e.g., "*cholesterol lowering drugs*" is also better then just *drugs*.
- Know ahead of time any important buzzwords or jargon that is used in the industry or subject field. For example, if you're looking for articles on wireless Internet, you might include the phrase "*hot spots.*"
- Try testing out your keywords on a free news search engine first (such as Google News or AltaVista News) to see what kind of results you receive. Read through a few retrieved articles that seem to be most relevant, and note what words or phrases occur most often in those items. Then redo your search using those words and phrases. Again, review the most promising results and see if there is once again the opportunity to add words to refine your search. Repeat this process a few times until you are satisfied that the results that you're retrieving are on target.

You should also take this opportunity to see if any words you are testing are causing false hits or causing irrelevant results to be retrieved. If you do find this to be the case, you can resolve this problem either by trying to find a substitute word or, if the alert service offers the option, you can use the Boolean NOT to eliminate any news items that include that word or phrase to appear in your results. (You need to be careful, though, when using the NOT operator because you do not want to eliminate relevant results too.)

On the matter of false hits, Comcowich at CyberAlert also warns "of searching on 'generic' terms" (especially if the company name is generic). He gave the example that "Mary Kay" is the name of a company, but many individuals have the same name. Instead, he advises, search on "Mary Kay" AND (company OR cosmetic OR beauty OR etc.). Similarly, Gary Stock of Nexcerpt advises that you test your keywords ahead of time to make sure that those words aren't also commonly used in other ways that you weren't aware of. This is a common cause of false hits when setting up an alert profile. For instance, are you looking for information on market trends in keyboards? Well, if you don't further qualify "keyboard," you'll get results related to both computer and piano keyboards.

Note, too, that several of the news alert services permit users to actually do some test searching and run some sample test searches on its news database. Testing a search on the actual alert service itself will give you an even better feel for what will likely turn out to be the best keywords and phrases. It will also give you a chance to try out advanced search features, which are discussed next.

Use Advanced Search Features

The next factor that will determine the effectiveness of your keywords is how you utilize (if you are permitted to utilize) certain advanced search features. As with the previous section, this information will be familiar to experienced researchers.

When creating your keyword profile, you should try to integrate as many of these advanced search features as possible:

- Use multiple word phrases where possible, and where appropriate.
- Use Boolean operators AND, OR, NOT where possible and appropriate, particularly the AND for narrowing a search.
- Where available, look for the Booleanlike NEAR or proximity operator, which allows you to specify that retrieved news items must not only contain your keywords, but that those keywords will be located close together (NEAR), or within the exact number of words apart that you specify (via a proximity operator).

Also take the opportunity to see what other limits or filters you can apply to your search to help make it more precise. Here are the most important ones to look for and consider using in your search profile:

- **Title/Headline.** Narrowing your alert profile so that only articles where your keywords appear in the title or headline of a news item is one of the best ways to ensure that the results retrieved are relevant and specific to your needs. This feature is particularly important if your search is a broad one and you are receiving lots and lots of results.
- **Industry.** Some alert services allow you to check off names of industries and will only return articles that relate to that specific industry.
- **Geographic.** When you are given this choice, you typically can choose to receive only those news items that originate from a particular state, country, or the world.
- **Subject.** This is an unusual filter, but when it is offered it can be a very powerful one, though it needs to be used carefully. Some alert services—primarily ones that we've categorized as the "traditional online vendor" services, assign a human to index each incoming news article by a specific subject code. This process helps ensure that the incoming item is truly about a certain topic, despite what particular words appear in the article. So if you can select a subject category, you will pretty much know for a fact that all incoming articles you receive will be about just that specific subject. (You just need to be sure that by limiting your

incoming news to that subject category, you aren't missing other important relevant items that might fall under another category.)

- **Source Type.** Among the kinds of news sources that an alert service might scan are online newspapers, journals, discussion groups, broadcasts, and blogs. You should look carefully to make sure that you will be getting incoming news from the kind of news sources you want to monitor. So, for instance, if your news alert provider includes blogs, but you don't want to get news from blogs, you should ideally have an option to exclude that news category from your alert.

- **Source Grouping.** Some news alert services will group together related sources by some useful category. For example, the Nexcerpt alert service groups all of its news titles into 33 subject "themes." Factiva Track Module offers something called Editor's Choice—which are the publications that Factiva's editors have chosen to be the best within their industry category.

- **Specific Title.** Some alert services allow their users to browse a listing of all of the news source titles included and check off which specific ones to include or exclude. This feature can be very useful if you are getting lots of irrelevant results from a certain title, or if you just want to set up a narrowly targeted search just to monitor, say, a handful or a few dozen of your very favorite news sources.

Advanced alert services, particularly those offered by the traditional online services, like Dialog, LexisNexis, and Factiva, will offer even more field searches and limits such as author's name, date of publication, words that appear in a summary/abstract, and so forth.

Once you have created what you feel is a search profile that includes the best keywords, employs advanced search functions, and is limited to the appropriate fields, you should try to give that search a test run right on the site, as discussed earlier, in order to assess the results and see if any further modifications are necessary before making the profile final.

Tip: Look for a "Remove Duplicates" Option

One of the biggest problems with news alerts is receiving multiple versions of the same article. This problem occurs most often with stories that go out over one of the newswires, as these stories are picked up by literally thousands of print and online newspapers and news sources. Some news alert services try to detect and remove duplicates automatically (by comparing headlines and other distinguishing characteristics), but success with this process varies. Some alert services by default will send duplicates, but offer a "remove duplicates" checkbox on the options page for users that don't want duplicate stories. Unless you need to track each time a different media source carries the same story (as some in the public relations industry need to do), we would highly recommend clicking a "remove duplicate" box if one is offered.

Set Your Delivery Preferences

All news alert services, from the simplest to the most complex, allow users to decide exactly how the alerts will be sent. While these decisions are not as critical as the creation of a good search profile, they are still important in that they will effect how valuable and useful the service turns out. Here are the most important of these options, and some considerations in making a decision.

- **Timing of Delivery.** Choices typically include: Real-time/Immediate; 1/day; or several times per day. Factors to consider in making a decision: How critical is it that you are alerted to breaking news instantly? The downside of getting immediate alerts is that you'll get each news item sent to you in a separate e-mail, adding more items to your e-mail box. It can also be distracting to think about regularly having to check e-mails for immediate alerts.

- Format. You'll likely have a choice of receiving your alerts in HTML or plain text. Factors to consider: aesthetics—you won't see any graphic elements with just plain text. It's easy to click on a hotlink in an HTML e-mail vs. having to cut and paste any text URLs into your browser. But you need to be sure that your e-mail program supports HTML.
- Amount of News Article Sent. Choices typically include: headline only, headline with abstract, or headline with full text. At a minimum, be sure you ask to view the excerpt/abstract so you can determine whether or not the item is likely to be relevant enough for you to take the time to review the full article.

Evaluating Your Results

You now have your alert profile set up and running. You can just sit back and wait for the news items to start rolling in. Maybe!

If you're lucky and there have been no system glitches, you'll typically start seeing the first of the alerts in your e-mail within 24 hours. But if you don't receive anything at all after that time frame, you'll need to see what's going on. There are actually several reasons why you might not be receiving your alerts:

- There was a technical problem in setting up your alert.
- The system is working, but there haven't been any news items that matched your keywords. The best alert services will send you an e-mail each day (or at whatever interval you specified) anyway, to let you know that no results were received. This at least lets you know that everything is working the way it should be.
- The alerts are going to a different/wrong e-mail address.
- Your e-mail software is viewing the incoming alerts as spam and either deleting them or forwarding them to a spam, bulk mail, or other kind of folder designated for unwanted e-mail.

You'll need, then, to check with the alert vendor to ensure that you are indeed getting the alerts as you expected.

Once you *are* getting your alerts, you'll be in the position to determine whether you're getting the kind of articles and news items that you were hoping to receive. If you've set your alert service to send you news items as they are breaking, they will come in one by one and you will likely see some hint of what the article is about in the header of the e-mail message (unless you've set a preference so that all items are grouped as a single e-mail—in that case, you'll probably just get a nondescript header like: Alerts for June 1 2004).

Based on the header, you may decide to open or not open the e-mail. Once opened, if you have set your preferences as recommended, you should get enough bibliographic and summary information to determine whether or not you'd like to go to the actual news item and read the full text. As you begin assessing the relevance and quality of what you are getting, you'll probably want to note certain matters on the news items that turn out to be most relevant, such as:

- What kind of sources—Web sites, digital versions of print articles, online newspapers, discussion groups, etc., are providing the best results? Conversely, which types may be giving you false or irrelevant results?
- Which keywords are retrieving the best hits? Which aren't working at all, or are working poorly?

(If you are rolling the alert service out to a larger group, you may wish to do a quick e-mail survey with a couple open-ended questions in order to obtain feedback from the individuals in the group.)

Based on the initial assessment of these matters, you should now go back and make any adjustments to your keywords as well as to your preferences to see if your search couldn't be tweaked a bit more.

At this point, you should also consider actually speaking with a technical or customer service representative at the alert firm to receive some assistance in further fine-tuning your search. The ability to work with an actual person at the alert service firm, and the quality of the help that you obtain will vary quite a bit among vendors. A lot depends on whether the alert service is free or a premium fee-based one. The former offers little or no personal assistance, while the latter may provide quite a bit, particularly if it is a firm with which you already have some kind of subscription in place. In any case, it is at least worth trying to make the contact, as you can save yourself a great deal of time hunting for the right tweaks and help pages on the site by shortcutting the process and talking to a helpful expert at the firm.

Integrating Alerts Into Your Workflow

Many of us view news alerts as a way to get a handle on the enormous amount of digital information that's available today. Judiciously used, news alerts can indeed be part of a full personal and organizational information management plan. But it's also very easy to get into a situation where alerts become just a few more (or hundreds more!) pieces of annoying, irrelevant bits of information that come flying at us each day—more like an assault than a savior.

We discuss the specific issue of avoiding "news alert overload" in a later section. First we will mention a few important tips on how to be a smarter user of alert services so that what you receive will be well integrated into your day-to-day workflow.

1. Be certain you've followed all the previous advice on making sure that your search profile is going to retrieve news items that are likely to be as relevant as possible and delivered just the way you want them. It won't make sense to create an effective system to view information that's not useful to you!

Tip: Using Multiple Alerts

Gary Stock of Nexcerpt told us that in order to manage his alert news reading time more effectively, sometimes he sets up *two* alerts on the same topic: One is an extremely precise alert that will only retrieve a few extremely targeted results; the other is a broader alert set up to obtain lots of results. Stock says that if he sees any new results in the very precise one, he will almost always click on it to read the results, since any news items captured by that query are likely to be very relevant and important. Then, if he has the time, he will go into the broader folder and scan those items to find other useful results.

Setting up two queries like this provides two advantages. Not only does it provide more options and flexibility in determining how much time you need to spend reviewing the alerts, but by creating both a narrow and broad search, it also helps create another filter for sorting your results.

2. Think about where you want these news alerts to "go" as they arrive. Since they will be e-mail based, there's no way around the fact that you are going to get more e-mail. What you want to avoid, though, is:

1. Having these alerts get lost among the rest of your e-mail.
2. Getting too many or getting them too often.
3. Not having a plan on what to do with the valuable articles once you read and open them.

On the first point, the most important piece of advice is to be sure that your incoming alerts are *not* mixed in with the rest of your regular e-mail. Depending on the kind of e-mail software you are using, you can accomplish this cordoning off of your news alerts by taking one of these options:

- Create a brand new separate e-mail address that is *only* dedicated to receiving your incoming news alerts (AOL users can do this easily by creating a new screen name, but anyone can do this by creating a new free account on a service like HotMail or Yahoo!).
- Many organizational users will not be able to create a consumer e-mail address, of course, and will need to integrate the incoming alerts into the firm's own e-mail system. In this case, what you need to do, either as the administrator for a larger group, or for your own personal e-mail box, is to find out how to create special folders in your e-mail program so that the incoming news alerts will automatically be directed into them. Each e-mail program works differently, so you will need to set this up either by reviewing the help files yourself or asking an internal IT person for assistance.

An even more effective and advanced step, if your e-mail program permits it, would be to set up those folders and then apply word filters to the incoming alert e-mails. This way, not only do the incoming alerts have their own folder, but they are further filtered by being directed to subfolders based on what words are found in the alert's title or body.

One caution in the use of folders is that because you don't automatically view the individual e-mails in them when checking your regular e-mail box, the alerts can suffer from an "out of sight, out of mind" syndrome. It's easy to just ignore or forget about those e-mails that are relegated to folders out of your main view.

There are a couple of solutions to this. If your e-mail software allows it, you can use a word filter to identify the most urgent words, and if an incoming alert contains those words, you could have it delivered to your regular e-mail box. If this is not possible, you could always create an "urgent alerts" folder and then have those most critical ones delivered to that folder. Then, on a regular basis, you could check to see if anything has been delivered to that particular folder.

If your e-mail software cannot do word filtering, then you will need to be sure to set a certain time each day where you automatically scan those folders to check for incoming e-mail alerts.

If you are using an e-mail alert that is specifically designed for use over an intranet, than you as an administrator will likely have many other advanced options for creating group folders for established groups or new groups in your organization. Here you'll need to work closely with both your own internal staff and the alert vendor to make sure that you have been able to create the right folders for the right groups of people in your organization.

After you view an article, you then of course want to make sure that you don't lose track of it so that you'll be able to access it easily in the future when you need it. If you are part of a larger organization with an intranet or some kind of internal network, you most likely have some organizationwide system for storing and later accessing articles and news items, and you should make sure the articles you view from the alerts are integrated into this system. If you are accessing the articles on your own, you will need to set up your own personal folder storage and retrieval system.

One option for storing Web news pages is to use a Web page capture, search, and retrieval software program. One that was reviewed very positively in *The Information Advisor* is called SurfSaver. Although there are competitors, this product offered particularly useful features. Among them was the ability to not only capture and store Web pages, but to make annotations before saving the page and allow full text searching of the stored text on the Web page as well as the annotations. You can sign up for a free trial of SurfSaver at its Web site (www.surfsaver.com).

The bottom line, then, to keep in mind is:

- Separate incoming alert e-mails from your regular e-mail.
- Use folders and/or word filters to help organize and group incoming alerts into categories.
- Make sure you set up a system where you will regularly review the incoming alerts.
- Work with any internal groups on setting up folders.
- Create a method for storing and easily retrieving the actual news items themselves.

Evaluating Usefulness and Credibility of the Information

Today, there has been an explosion of sites on the Web that offer news in some fashion. There are, for example, Web companion sites to well-known print newspapers and broadcasters (e.g., the *LA Times*, *The New York Times*, *USA Today*, CNN, MSNBC, and the BBC); there are news and information sites that have built a reputation and have a large audience but are original to the Web and have no print version (e.g., CNET, ZDNet, Slate, Salon); and there are pure aggregators (Yahoo! News, Google News, NewsNow) that collect articles from thousands of news sources on the Web and permit users to search its database. While not technically considered a "news site" per se, some alert services also include conversation posts from discussion groups. And, most recently, there are the bloggers.

While the topic of how to evaluate the credibility and quality of news sources on the Web is beyond the scope of this report, there is such a deluge of news on the Web these days that we think it would be appropriate to make a few comments on the matter of online news credibility.

Below are some questions to consider when coming across an unfamiliar news source on the Internet, as well as a few active steps you can take to help ascertain the credibility of a particular Web-based news source.

Questions to Consider When Assessing the Credibility of an Unknown News Source on the Internet

- Is there a print equivalent to this Web-based news source?
  - To find out: Check a standard print reference directory in your library, such as *Gale Directory of Publications and Broadcast Media*, *Ulrich's International Periodicals Directory*, or *Editor & Publisher's International Yearbook*.
- How long has this source been publishing? What is the mission/purpose/agenda of this source?
  - To find out: Look for an "about us" link on the news page to read about the history and background of the source. Other useful links to read that can provide additional background are a media/press/news link to scan recent press releases and links to other online news sites that have written about this source.
- What is the popular reputation of this source?
  - To find out: Search for mentions of its name on a standard search engine like Google, on discussion groups (such as Google News), and on blog search engines (such as Daypop).

- Who is on the staff? What is their background?
  - To find out: Look for an "about us" link on the site to read about who is behind this source.
- What is the background/experience of the writer of the article?
  - To find out: Do a Web search on the author's name to find out his/her other associations and where else he or she has been published.
- Where is this source located? How can you contact it?
  - To find out: Look for an "about us" link on the site for full contact information. Sometimes you can also find this information under "press," "media relations/press relations," or "investor relations."
- What are the ramifications for this source if it has passed along bad information?
  - To find out: Consider whether this source is a very large, well-known news organization with a vast audience or a tiny niche news site. Is it more like an MSNBC or Mike's Rants on Raccoons? The point is that the biggest news organizations are likely to employ editors, proofreaders, and fact checkers. Because they are well-known and watched carefully, what they publish is more likely to get scrutiny than a tiny unknown site, so they may pay more attention to the ramifications of publishing bad information. This principle is true for bloggers too—the biggest and most well-known ones are more likely to hear about their errors than the really obscure ones.
- Where else is this source referenced or cited?
  - To find out: Search on the source's name on a Web search engine. Find out who else links to it (via the "who links to" function on a search engine like Google or AlltheWeb.com).

Some Proactive Steps You Might Take to Assess an Unknown News Site's Credibility

- Contact the publication yourself to get a sense of its operation and staffing.
- E-mail the author of an article you are assessing with your own follow-up questions.
- "Google" the publication to find out what others are saying about it.
- Search a traditional database to see if anyone has written about that source in a trade publication.
- Spend some time on the site, and look at some factors that indicate attention to detail. Check to see:
  - How recently the site was updated.
  - If the various search and navigation features work as they should.
  - If there is a customer service link that works.
  - If it looks like attention has been paid to a modern, sleek design and interface.
  - If background information is provided on the publisher, including ownership, history, mission, staffing, and how to best use the source.

Finally, you should read through some of the source's recent articles and notes to its readers so you can find out if all the articles reflect a similar point of view, political philosophy, or position on a contentious issue. This will help you judge its reports in that larger context.

The Blog Factor

While not all news alert services include blogs, a couple do. It appears that as the popularity of blogs increases, they will be included in more news alert services. This presents new challenges for online news readers.

Blogs have been a mixed blessing for information gatherers. On the one hand, many bloggers have done researchers a great favor by opening up and expanding the media ecosystem. They've added fresh voices that were previously ignored or overlooked by the traditional mainstream media; have made personal, grassroots contributions that provide unique eyewitness reports to newsworthy events; and have brought up stories that were missed by the general media or expanded on stories in the news with additional research, linking, and discussion among bloggers.

But the downside to blogs and this kind of personal journalism is pretty obvious. How do you know if the person is telling the truth or passing along accurate information? What if the blogger has some undisclosed nefarious agenda? What's a researcher to do?

In our view, blogs *are* potentially legitimate sources of news. In the course of researching some topics that we follow for *The Information Advisor*, we personally have had the experience of finding some of the best insights and most cutting-edge thinking from bloggers.

However, these sources must be used very carefully. The key, in using blogs as a source of news, is to slowly build up a small collection of trusted bloggers that you come to feel can be replied upon. Today the key to cutting through news and information overload is to have a handful of sources that you feel are effective filters for what you need to know, and whom you trust, and that would include bloggers as well.

This brings up the obvious question—how do you know which bloggers to trust? In many ways, coming to trust a blogger is not that much different from coming to trust, say, a certain columnist in a print newspaper or journal that you regularly read and whose work you've come to appreciate over time. You are introduced to the person's writings, are impressed with what you've read, check that person's column again in the future, are impressed again, and so you make a regular effort to keep up with that person's work.

One difference, though, in using bloggers as trusted sources vs. relying on a newspaper columnist is that with bloggers, there are no preliminary *institutional* screens or filters to assist you in making this judgment. In other words, you don't have the luxury of scanning a newspaper or journal that you already know and trust to look for good writers. In those cases, the columnists you find have already passed the hurdle of being good enough to write for that publication. Because bloggers are typically not associated with a larger publishing enterprise, you'll need to put additional effort into determining which ones you want in your circle of trusted information sources.

In Blogs We Trust?

Is there a guide to determining who to trust? Deciding to place your trust in a particular person is, of course, a kind of gut feeling that cannot be completely dissected and analyzed. However, it's worth thinking about why one might choose to place trust in a particular individual's veracity as an information source. *The Information Advisor* published an article on trust and news sources online (*The Information Advisor*, September 2003), and there we discussed the factors that typically lead one to trust an individual as an information source. We noted that trust is placed in a person when her or she:

- Has proven to be reliable and accurate in the past and has built a track record.
- Is more concerned with the integrity of the issue under examination than competing concerns (such as the impact of his/her views on advancing a career, political appearances, appeasing higher powers, etc.).
- Writes in a manner that displays fresh insights that clarify the subject and ultimately increase your own understanding.
- Is immersed in the field he/she is commenting on.
- Embodies values that correspond to your own.

One nice thing about using bloggers as trusted sources is that once you have found one that you like, you can often readily find the names of other bloggers that *that*

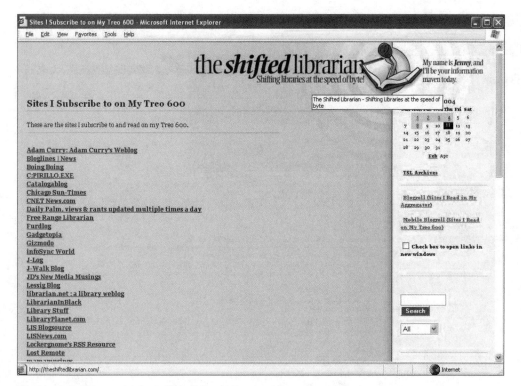

The blogroll of Jenny Levine's The Shifted Librarian blog

person has confidence in and relies on, since many bloggers post a "blogroll"—links to other bloggers that they like and recommend. If you link to those bloggers, then they may often have their own blogroll too, providing you with additional potentially good sources. Naturally, after a certain point this process of tracking down and reviewing linked bloggers becomes self-defeating and potentially never-ending! But you can begin to refine your set of favorite bloggers by taking this tack.

If you like a particular blogger's commentary on some topic, you can also use the "TrackBack" function at the end of the blogger's posting to find the names of other bloggers who linked to and/or commented on that post. This can be another good strategy for finding other blogs that may be worth reading.

A site that helps identify incoming bloggers on a much broader scale is Technorati, which monitors and indexes over 1.8 million blogs and RSS feeds, updating them, according to the site owners, every 9 minutes. Technorati ranks bloggers and even specific conversation threads based on how many other bloggers and online news sites are linking to that topic or blog. It also ranks the most "talked about" news, current events, and books on its indexed sites. Technorati also offers "Watchlists," which are customized reports that track incoming links to specified blogs, news, and Web sites.

Finding Trusted Bloggers

How do you actually locate a good blogger in the first place? Well, you may be referred to a blog in an article from a standard print journal that quotes a blogger (reporters make nice filters here in weeding out the most prominent bloggers on a subject). You might also come across a blogger's site as a hit in a search on Google or another Web search engine. There are also search engines that only search blogs—two good ones are Daypop (www.daypop.com) and WayPath (www.waypath.com).

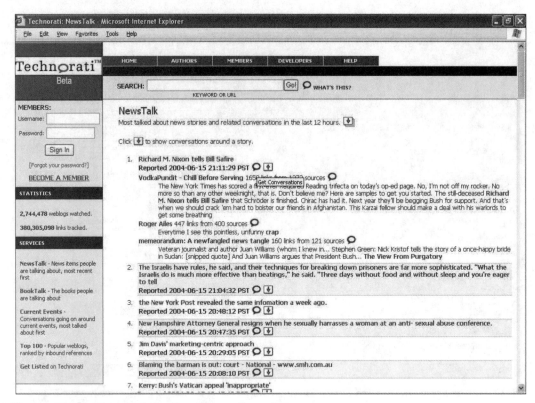

Technorati ranks the popularity of specific postings of bloggers

When you initially link to a blogger's site, you'll want to assess the quality of the blog. This assessment will be easiest if you already know something about the topic, because you should be able to size up the knowledge and abilities of the blogger pretty quickly.

If you're uncertain about the credibility of a particular blogger or blogging post that you've come across, you certainly don't want to rely on it or pass along information, unverified, to others. However, you may not wish to necessarily dismiss what you find on the other hand either. Instead, we would advise that you view any information, statistics, news reports, and opinions, as possible *leads*, as a reporter would. If that information is potentially significant, you should perform your own checks and research to see if other sources confirm that information, and if necessary, go to any cited original source itself as a final verification step.

The Internet Trust Matrix

On the Internet, the matrix of trust is built around the referral—who is recommending whom, and who is linking to one's site or blog. Some sites, like the consumer advisor site Epinions, even have its members create a specific network of trusted Epinion reviewers (Epinions calls this its "web of trust"), whose opinions will be given higher rankings. Epinions will also try to find other members with the same individuals in *their* web of trust and make an assumption that other people in those people's trust circle are more likely to be people you are more likely to trust as well.

Tip: Confirming or Debunking Urban Legends and Hoaxes

The Internet serves as a great rumor creation and dissemination mechanism, and countless claims, charges, and strange stories circulate via e-mail, bloggers, and discussion groups. It can be very difficult to determine just how true these stories are: Did Latin American car buyers really avoid buying Chevy Novas because "no va" translates as "doesn't go" in Spanish? (No). Did Starbucks really close all its stores in Israel? (Yes). Can cell phone usage cause explosions near gas pumps? (No fully confirmed incidents, but there may be a real but tiny risk factor.)

Luckily, there are sites on the Web that are devoted specifically to getting to the bottom of some of the more widespread of these circulating stories. They provide answers as to whether or not the stories are true, false, or simply uncertain. Here are the names of two of the leading sites that perform this valuable function:

Urban Legends Reference Page: www.snopes.com

About.Com: Urban Legends and Folklore: urbanlegends.about.com/

Finally, when you do settle on bloggers that you like and trust, you will probably want to keep up with their postings. If that blogger's site is not included as a source in your news alert service (or cannot be added as a custom request), you should consider other ways to keep up, such as subscribing to the blogger's RSS Feed or a Web page watcher-type software, as described earlier in this report.

Case Study: Checking an Unverified Claim about Microcars

We recently had to do some research online on an interesting and quirky kind of topic—why is it that the teeny little cars that are so popular in Europe are not available in the U.S.? In searching the Web, we came across an online forum called Allpar, which describes itself as a site that "serves Dodge, Chrysler, Plymouth, DeSoto, and Jeep owners and enthusiasts." Members on this group discussed developments, trends, and issues that affected owners of those cars. We noted that the site owner posted a tip passed along from a couple of its members, informing the group that DaimlerChrysler was going to be bringing its tiny "Smart Car," which has been quite the rage in Europe over the last few years, to the United States in 2006, and would be doing so by using an existing manufacturing plant located in Juiz de Fora, Brazil. This was interesting news and relevant to our research—if it was true. We then went about making an effort to use that tidbit as a lead for verification. Here are the few simple steps we took:

1. Because the posting identified the names of the members who passed along that tip, we did a search on the two persons' names to see what we could learn about their own background, and to assess their own credibility. It turned out that both people were actively involved in the automotive industry and were cited on other sites as good experts on various topics related to automobiles. A good sign—but not enough!

2. We then took the most specific/obscure phrase that was in that three paragraph posting and did an additional search on the Web. We searched on "Juiz de Fora" and added "Smart Car." This then led us to another car forum called "Automotive Intelligence" that repeated this same information. Another good sign, since this was a confirmation, though still not from a recognized source. Additional searches retrieved several "name" publications with a presence on the Web that repeated the same bit of news. Those sources included Motor Trend, Forbes, Business Week, and Bloomberg.

3. By now, we were convinced that this was very likely to be accurate information, which then gave us additional confidence in that initial source, as well as in the two individuals who made that first posting. They might be interesting experts to track down and interview if we needed to do so.

4. Although we did not pursue this in this instance, the next and final step would be to contact the automotive firm itself to confirm the accuracy of this information.

We could have approached confirming this information differently. For instance, we could have immediately called the automotive company to try to confirm the data, but given that it seemed that this was rumored information at the time, we were not confident that we could get a good answer. We could also have tried to track down the e-mails or phone numbers of the two forum members that posted the tip, and asked them our own questions to try to gauge their credibility. But ultimately, it was pretty easy to find several reliable confirming sources right on the Web, giving us a high degree of confidence that this was accurate information.

Some of this confidence also comes from the fact that those sources (Bloomberg, *Business Week*, and *Forbes*) would be considered of the highest level of trustworthiness for business researchers. For the names of other "core" news and information sources, see the Appendix.

The New Media Ecosystem

What counts as news, and how news is created and disseminated, has gotten a lot more interesting and a lot more complex over the last few years. Because of the Web, news today is generated not only top-down from producers, publishers, and editors, but frequently and increasingly, bottom-up from individuals with blogs and RSS feeds (alternative online news sites that employ a "participatory journalism" model where readers are also contributors) and, to a lesser degree, on online forums attached to larger news sites. The dynamic that takes place between these grassroots Web-based news sources and the traditional print and broadcast media is radically changing the way news is reported, how it flows, and how we receive it.

Although bloggers spend a lot of time discussing and complaining about events and issues that they feel are being ignored or overlooked by the mainstream media, reporters with traditional print and broadcast sites increasingly are trolling blogs and online news sites to look for fresh leads to find unreported stories or to try to take the pulse of what people are discussing online. Bloggers often rely on stories that are first reported in the mainstream press as jumping off points for making their own critiques and further expanding the issue in ways that they feel the topic should have been pursued by standard print newspapers and broadcast news.

All of this back and forth has created a very lively flow of information that continually travels back and forth between the bloggers/online news sites and the traditional media. This has had a couple of significant impacts on the news. For one, it has accelerated the news creation and dissemination cycle. Bloggers—who can post breaking news instantly and don't even need to be at their own computer to do so—have raised the bar on what it means to be first with a news story, and they have increased the pressure to be out faster with breaking news for all types of media. It also means that more nonmainstream views and opinions are making their way into the traditional media and, in some cases, have become integrated into stories as legitimate sources. Ultimately, all of this rather frenzied activity has been a good thing for information seekers, as it produces *more* information on *more* topics from *more* points of view.

But there are at least two major downsides to this phenomena. The first is simply the growing volume of online news. We discuss a few strategies on how to deal with this in the next section. The other problem is that with so much new news working its way from blogs and online news sites into the mainstream press, the odds increase that inaccurate information and, specifically, unfounded rumors that start on blogs and online news sites may not just be found on the Web, but work their way into the *mainstream* press.

A recent case where an unfounded rumor began seeping into the mainstream press occurred when a remark was posted on a rather infamous online news site, The Drudge Report. Though not technically a blog (Drudge does not use blogging software), The Drudge Report is a one-person, unfiltered news, rumor, and information site. In this case, Matt Drudge posted a rumor that mainstream media outlets were looking into a charge that John Kerry had had an affair with an intern. The rumor worked its way up the media ecology chain—picked up by tabloid magazines, conservative talk radio, overseas scandal-oriented newspapers, insider-type political publications, and then cable news outlets. The mainstream print press chose not to report these rumors, but the allegation generated enough under-the-radar buzz that Kerry was asked about it on a talk show (he denied the affair). The denial then made for a small mention in some major media outlets. Ultimately, the intern in question issued a full denial, and the case was essentially closed. (For more on this, see "Kerry rumor shows how scandal travels in the media," Mark Jurkowitz, *Boston Globe*, 2/23/2004, p. D9.)

While in this case the mainstream press chose not to print the rumor, the larger point that all news users need to keep in mind is that today the dynamics of the news industry are such that even some established trusted news sources are going to be reading blogs and are going to be exposed to more leads and rumors from bloggers. With competition to be first still driving much of the industry, some mainstream media outlets are likely to feel some pressure to report these questionable stories. Tom Rosenstiel, the director of the Project for Excellence in Journalism, an organization designed to raise journalistic standards, expressed the worry that what happens in this kind of situation is that "What you get is ... the bad journalism driving out the good." (*Boston Globe*, Jurkowitz, p. D9)

The best news organizations—in print and on the Web—will apply their existing ethical standards and principles to try to ensure that all rumors and unverified information be checked and confirmed before publication.

Avoiding News Alert Overload

One of the reasons that people sign up with a news alert service is to manage and cut down on information overload. Ironically, one of the biggest downsides of signing up with an e-mail news alert service is receiving *more* e-mail and *more* information.

The concept of using a news alert service to reduce information overload sounds good in theory, but, for several reasons, it doesn't always work out as planned. For one, as discussed earlier, if you make any errors in creating your profile, or don't fine-tune your keywords just right—you can receive a lot of irrelevant news. In fact, even a perfectly created news alert profile is still likely to bring back at least some irrelevant items, just because of the difficulties in getting back those stories that cover the concepts of what you "meant" you wanted to read about, vs. what your keywords literally retrieved. Right off the bat, you're unlikely to get anywhere near 90–100 percent relevancy from your alert service. (Note that a couple of news alert services, such as Burrelle's/Luce, specifically promote a feature whereby a human editor will review each incoming news item to be sure it really matches what its users want before sending the item along.)

In addition, you may find, especially if you are tracking a broad or popular topic, that you are getting lots and lots of e-mails cluttering up your e-mail box.

Finally, even if the items *are* mostly relevant, and you aren't being overwhelmed with too many e-mails, you may simply discover that there is a whole lot more good material on the topic that you are receiving than you realized and that you simply don't have the time to wade through all of these articles—even though they are valuable and relevant. This can be quite frustrating and have some debilitating psychological results: You know there is a lot of news that you "should" be reading—just waiting for you—but you aren't. From that, it can be a slippery slope to "I'm not being as productive as I should be ... I'm not doing my job well ..." and, if you really suffer from this, you get down to "so I'm a rotten person." Gee, all that distress just from signing up for an e-mail news alert service!

Well, we certainly don't want your self-esteem to suffer from something as trivial, in the grand scheme of things, as your news alerts. Here are a few tips on how to avoid suffering from this "news alert overload" syndrome:

- The worst kind of overload is to be overloaded with useless information, so be sure you've fine-tuned your keywords and used any advanced search features so that the items you retrieve are as relevant as possible.

- Avoid, if at all possible, creating broad news alert topics. The narrower and more obscure the better! News alerts are great for pinpointing when people, products, companies, and unusual topics are mentioned somewhere in the news. They are poorly suited for monitoring broad topics and issues.

- Remember to create separate alert e-mail folders and, if possible, word filters to organize your incoming alerts.

- If you are getting too many individual e-mails and you don't need to be alerted instantly when new news breaks, change your preferred delivery time from immediate/breaking to once or twice per day or to a "summary" option where all of the day's alerts are collected in a single e-mail.

- After the alerts have been running for a week or so, do a review of how they are working, get input from others who are receiving them, and find out if there are any specific news sources that are consistently not helpful, and look for an option to exclude them from your profile.

- Rather than worrying about unread e-mail news, pick a specific time of the day—perhaps at the very end of the day, or the very beginning, where you will allot, say, 15 minutes to review your alerts. If you find an article that seems valuable and worth reading in detail, save it to a folder. Set aside a specific 1- or 2-hour slot each week to read those saved articles (and forward any to others who need to see them). Of course, if you need to be alerted to breaking news as it happens, you don't have this luxury of waiting, though for most business researchers, such a need is uncommon.

- Try to identify which specific sources and which individual writers, columnists, and bloggers regularly offer the most valuable insights. When you are short on time (okay, that may be all the time), just look for and read the items from those sources. You might even consider, as a drastic but effective way to reduce news alert overload, to limit all alerts just to those few sources. You could even set up a keyword profile with the trusted person's name so that only articles written by (or that mention) that person are retrieved.

- Relax about what you might be missing. There's no possible way to keep up with any field completely these days. It's an impossible task, so the best you can do is to have a few trusted sources that you rely on serve as your filters, and review these when you get a chance.

A Plea to Bring Back MSNBC's Little Bullseye

One of the reasons that news alerts can increase, not decrease, information over-load is that we are already getting so many e-mails—way too many in most cases. Signing up to get more e-mails is something that one doesn't take lightly these days! But it is the standard way to get alerts to breaking and important news right away at your own desktop.

But is it the only way? For some time, MSNBC offered an alert service whereby a little bullseye icon would flash (and beep too, if you wanted) on your toolbar on your PC's desktop whenever a new news item came in that matched your keywords. You'd then click on that bullseye and view the incoming story. We had tested this MSNBC alert and found it an excellent way to deliver breaking news—you didn't need to be in your e-mail program to know that something important was coming in, the icon was noticeable but unobtrusive, and—most importantly—there were no extra e-mails to wade through!

Unfortunately, when MSNBC revamped its news alert service early in 2004 to a new MSN-backed service, it not only did away with keyword searches (which is why we do not cover the MSN service in this report), but also removed the icon method for alerting users. We think this is too bad—it was a real innovation that made a difference in helping to reduce e-mail clutter.

So, how about you other alert vendors reading this report—why not make this a new option for customers of your alert services?

Appendix

Core Business Sources

It seems like an obvious consideration, but it is easily overlooked—that the news alert service that you use is monitoring the highest quality news sources and those that are most important to you. You should be aware, then, which specific news sources you want to make sure you're tracking, which ones are considered leaders in your industry or field, and the names of any important new ones on the scene.[1]

If you are monitoring news in a field that you're already immersed in, the job of pinpointing important titles should not be too difficult. You probably already know the names of key information sources, and if you run a library or organization's information center, you can also do a quick survey of your staff to find out what others in your organization are relying on.

But what if you are planning on monitoring stories in an area that is unfamiliar to you, and you aren't sure which sources are the "must" ones?

How to Find the Best News Sources?

At the end of this section, you will see that we have compiled a kind of "generalists" list of the most important general business and trade information sources of interest to a wide range of businesspersons. There are more details about this selection and how to use it in that section.

Your own news monitoring needs are also likely to be quite specific, either based on an industry or subindustry that you need to track, a region of the world, a certain technology trend, or perhaps some specific legal or regulatory matter. In any case, you would want to try to ensure that your alert service includes those particular sources—or, if it doesn't, that you are accessing these important sources through some other means.

Although some basic research and test Web searching is one way to try to locate names of leading news and information sources for an unfamiliar field, one way to get a quick and authoritative recommendation of key publications in a specific subject or industry is to consult the invaluable directory, *Katz's Magazines for Libraries* (Bowker, 12th ed., December 2003). The book, which can be found in most libraries, identifies and carefully describes what the authors, who are primarily librarians, have determined are the absolute "must" news and information sources for hundreds of different subject areas ranging from aeronautics and Africa to waste treatment and Zambia. It's worth noting, too, that the latest editions of the directory include not just print sources, but sources that are on the Web as well.

Does the Alert Vendor Include Them?

There's good news and bad news when it comes to figuring out whether a news alert vendor includes your "must" sources. The bad news is that many news alert vendors don't make it easy, or don't reveal the titles of the sources that they are covering in their alert services. So it won't necessarily be obvious from the get-go as to who covers what source.

On the bright side, though, some vendors will add new news sources suggested by its users. Some vendors have said that, if the source is a free Web-based one, that they would seriously consider *adding* that source's URL to its own news crawl.

Furthermore, as mentioned earlier, you should keep in mind that a smart business news consumer does not only rely on a news alert service as a "balanced" news diet. Alert services can serve an excellent function for staying on top of timely news events, but because most news alert services are focused on Web-sources or online newspapers, you won't be getting many in-depth features, analyses, and longer, more analytical pieces as you'd find in trade and academic journals.

With that said, let's now look at the list that we've put together to represent 100+ "core" business news and information sources. It's pretty obvious that there is no such thing as one perfect general list of "critical" business news and information sources for everyone. Each of us has our own specific needs and preferences in a source, and it's up to each of us to determine what those are and try to ensure that we are accessing those sources—either as part of a news alert service, by searching them on an online service, or even by a good old print subscription!

Even though we all need to come up with our own personalized listing of the best information sources, there still exist some general business news sources that have come to be seen as the leaders in their field, publishing consistently valuable and insightful pieces. They are considered the trend and agenda setters for their area.

What are those sources? We endeavored to come up with such a list, and it is published in two parts in Source List 1 and Source List 2. Although our primary purpose in compiling these titles was to help you determine which business core sources are included in a particular vendor's alerting product, this list could also prove to be useful as a way to identify sources you may wish to be reviewing on a regular basis.

How did we arrive at this list? The initial step was to check and compare existing recommendations of core business titles from multiple credible sources. Those sources were:

- Two print directories:
  - *Katz's Magazines for Libraries*
  - *The Basic Business Library.*
- A survey of a selection of core business sources recommended by FIND/SVP's industry consultants.
- A review of the recommendations of an excellent reference guide created by the business library at the University of Florida, Gainesville (http://www.uflib.ufl.edu/businesslibrary/journals/busjournals.htm). Thanks to Peter McKay, business librarian at U. Florida for creating such an outstanding list.
- Queries to the BUSLIB (business librarians) and SLABF (SLA's business/ finance division) online discussion list.

We then identified those titles that were mentioned by more than one of these sources: Those that were mentioned the most frequently were culled for this list. Finally, we supplemented this list with some titles of our own, which are personal favorites, as well as the results of some additional online searching.

The result, then, is not a definitive all-purpose list but, we believe, a reasonable compilation of core business titles.

The list is broken down into two parts. Source List 1 contains the top 100 print-based business sources, which may or may not have a Web equivalent. Source List 2 includes 63 strictly Web-based business/general news sources.

Endnote

1. For some people, and for some kinds of news monitoring, the actual sources monitored may actually *not* be so critical. This is the case if you are only interested in being alerted to the really big news stories that are covered by virtually every major business news publication. When major news occurs, it will be picked up by at least one of the major wire services like AP or Reuters. If the news is big, those wire story reports will be published by thousands of news items. Ultimately, it doesn't matter that much whether you read that wire story from, say, BusinessWeek.com or Bloomberg.

Source List 1

One Hundred Key Print-Based Business News Sources

- *Academy of Management Journal*
- *Across the Board*
- *Administrative Science Quarterly*
- *Advertising Age*
- *Adweek*
- *Air Conditioning, Heating & Refrigeration News*
- *American Banker*
- *American Demographics*
- *American Economic Review*
- *Automotive News*
- *Aviation Week & Space Technology*
- *Barron's*
- *Bests Report*
- *Beverage Industry*
- *Beverage World*
- *Brandweek*
- *Broadcasting & Cable*
- *Business & Society*
- *Business & Society Review*
- *Business 2.0*
- *Business Communication Quarterly*
- *Business Ethics Quarterly*
- *Business History Review*
- *Business Horizons*
- *Business Week*
- *California Management Review*
- *Chain Store Age*
- *Chemical Market Reporter*
- *Chemical Week*
- *Chicago Tribune*
- *Christian Science Monitor*
- *Dealerscope*
- *Decision Sciences*
- *DSN Retailing*
- *Economist (UK)*
- *Electronic Business*
- *ENR: Engineering News Record*
- *Euromoney*
- *Fast Company*
- *Financial Times (UK)*
- *Footwear News*
- *Forbes*
- *Fortune*
- *Guardian*
- *Harvard Business Review*
- *Hotel and Motel Management*
- *Household and Personal Products*
- *HR Focus*
- *Human Relations*
- *Inc.*
- *Industrial and Corporate Change*
- *Industrial and Labor Relations Review*
- *Industry Week*
- *INFOR: Information Systems and Operational Research*
- *Information and Management*
- *Journal of Business Ethics*
- *Journal of Business Research*
- *Journal of Consumer Research*
- *Journal of Finance*
- *Journal of International Business Studies*
- *Journal of Management Information Systems*
- *Journal of Marketing Research*
- *Journal of Operations Management*

- *Journal of Organizational Behavior*
- *Journal of Retailing*
- *Journal of World Business*
- *Library Journal*
- *Long Range Planning*
- *Los Angeles Times*
- *Management & Marketing*
- *Management Science*
- *Marketing*
- *MIS Quarterly*
- *MIT Sloan Management Review*
- *Multinational Business Review*
- *New York Times*
- *Operations Research*
- *Organizational Dynamics*
- *Packaging Digest*
- *Personnel Psychology*
- *Platts*
- *Progressive Grocer*
- *Restaurant Business*
- *Retail Merchandiser*
- *Sales and Marketing Management*
- *San Jose Mercury News*
- *Searcher*
- *Strategy and Leadership*
- *Technology Review*
- *Telephony*
- *Textile World*
- *Thunderbird International Business Review*
- *Training*
- *Travel Weekly*
- *USA Today*
- *Variety*
- *Wall Street Journal*
- *Washington Post*
- *Wired Magazine*
- *Women's Wear Daily*

Source List 2

Key Web-Based
Business News Sources

Atlanta Journal-Constitution
www.ajc.com/

BBC World News
news.bbc.co.uk/

Bloomberg
www.bloomberg.com

Boston Globe
www.boston.com

Business 2.0
www.business2.com/

Business Times of Singapore
business-times.asia1.com.sg/

BusinessWeek.com
www.businessweek.com

BusinessWire
www.businesswire.com

C-SPAN
www.c-span.org/

CBC News
www.cbc.ca/news/

CBS MarketWatch
cbs.marketwatch.com/

Canada NewsWire
www.newswire.ca/en/

CFO
www.cfo.com/

Chicago Sun-Times
www.suntimes.com/

Chicago Tribune
www.chicagotribune.com/

Christian Science Monitor
www.csmonitor.com/

CIO
www.cio.com

CNBC
www.cnbc.com

CNET
www.cnet.com

CNN
www.cnn.com

CNNFN
www.money.cnn.com

Crain's
www.crainsny.com/

DarwinMag.com
www.darwinmag.com

DOWJONES.com
www.djnewswires.com

Economist
www.economist.com

Fast Company
www.fastcompany.com

Financial Times
www.ft.com

Forbes
www.forbes.com

Fortune
www.fortune.com

FOX News
www.foxnews.com

Globe and Mail
www.globeandmail.com

Guardian
www.guardian.co.uk/

Herald Tribune
www.iht.com/

Investor's Business Daily
www.investors.com/

Journal of Commerce
www.joc.com

Kiplinger
www.kiplinger.com

Los Angeles Times
www.latimes.com

Miami Herald
www.miami.com

MIT Tech Review
www.techreview.com/

MSN Money
moneycentral.msn.com/investor/home.asp

MSNBC
www.msnbc.com

Newsday
www.newsday.com

New York Post
www.nypost.com

New York Times
www.nytimes.com

NPR
www.npr.org

PBS
www.pbs.org

PR Newswire
www.prnewswire.com

Red Herring
www.redherring.com

Reuters
www.reuters.com

Salon
www.salon.com

Salt Lake Tribune
www.sltrib.com/

San Jose Mercury News
www.mercurynews.com

Search Engine Watch
www.searchenginewatch.com

TechNewsWorld
www.technewsworld.com/

Times Online
www.timesonline.co.uk/

Toronta Star
www.thestar.com/

USA TODAY
www.usatoday.com

VentureWire
www.venturewire.com

washingtonpost.com
www.washingtonpost.com

Wired News
www.wired.com

World Press Review
www.worldpress.org

Yahoo! News
dailynews.yahoo.com/

ZDNet
www.zdnet.com/

News Alert Service
Coverage of Core Business Sources

Vendor Source Comparison Tables

The following tables identify which of the 150 or so core business news sources we've identified are covered by which of the news alert services covered in this report. In order to allow you to compare like vendors with like, we've created the same kinds of categories for the tables as we've done for the rest of the report. Specifically, that means that we have created four separate tables, as follows:

- Free news alert services
- Inexpensive news alert services
- Fee-based/premium news alert services
- Traditional online news alert services

For each of the tables we have listed the two sets of core business news sources: those that are primarily found in print, and those that are primarily or only found on the Web. By reading across the rows, you can identify which alert service in its category includes which specific titles.

In order to make these tables more precise, we have used some abbreviations, as follows (note that the lists run consecutively within the tables):

List 1: Print Sources. If a vendor includes a title, it will be indicated by a "P" or a "W" in the cell. A "P" indicates that the vendor receives a digital feed created from the print publication, and this feed may come directly from the publisher or an aggregator. A "W" in the cell indicates that the vendor accesses a Web site version of the publication. Note that Web-based versions are not necessarily exactly the same as the original print source.

List 2: Web-based Sources. If a vendor includes one of these Web-based titles, it will be indicated by an "X." However, some vendors include the source but do not actually access it from the Web itself, but via a digital feed. In those cases, we indicate coverage with the abbreviation of "DF."

A few guidelines and advice in using these tables: First, not every vendor was able to provide us with their source listing. Second, keep in mind that while we believe we have compiled a useful, representative collection of what could be considered core business news sources, there is of course no one such perfect list, and what may be critical for one person could be quite optional for another. You'll want, of course, to identify any other key print or Web-based sources that are critical for you and find out which vendors include it. (In cases where you can simply browse a vendor's listing of sources right on the Web, we've provided a URL. In other cases, you will have to ask the vendor directly for an answer as to whether a particular title or set of titles is included.)

You'll see a few patterns in this chart. In general, the free and cheap services rely more on Web-based sources, while the more expensive ones integrate the print-based trade journals. You'll also find some sources that are included by just about everyone (the newswires, popular online newspapers), and a few that are quite rare to find. The fact that some sources are rare or impossible to find in full text via a news alert service is also a good reminder that these services should not be your only source of business news and information.

TABLE 1:
FREE NEWS ALERT SERVICES

- **American City Business Journals: Search Watch**
  (Not included in chart as this site only includes regional business journals.)
- **CBS MarketWatch: Keyword News Alert**
- **Google News Alert**
- **Yahoo! Alerts**

Core Business Journal Title Coverage

Type	Title	CBS MarketWatch: Keyword News Alert	Google News Alerts	YAHOO! Alerts
Print	Academy of Management Journal			
Print	Across the Board			
Print	Administrative Science Quarterly			
Print	Advertising Age			
Print	Adweek			
Print	Air Conditioning, Heating & Refrigeration News			
Print	American Banker			
Print	American Demographics			
Print	American Economic Review			
Print	Automotive News			
Print	Aviation Week & Space Technology			
Print	Barron's			
Print	Bests Review			
Print	Beverage Industry			
Print	Beverage World			
Print	Brandweek			
Print	Broadcasting & Cable			
Print	Business & Society			
Print	Business & Society Review			
Print	Business 2.0			
Print	Business Communication Quarterly			
Print	Business Ethics Quarterly			
Print	Business History Review			
Print	Business Horizons			
Print	Business Week			
Print	California Management Review			
Print	Chain Store Age			
Print	Chemical Marketing Reporter			
Print	Chemical Week			
Print	Chicago Tribune			
Print	Christian Science Monitor			
Print	Dealerscope			
Print	Decision Sciences			
Print	DSN Retailing			
Print	Economist (U.K.)			
Print	Electronic Business			
Print	ENR: Engineering News Record			
Print	Euromoney			

Type	Title	CBS MarketWatch: Keyword News Alert	Google News Alerts	YAHOO! Alerts
Print	Fast Company			
Print	Financial Times (U.K.)			
Print	Footwear News			
Print	Forbes			
Print	Fortune			
Print	Guardian			
Print	Harvard Business Review			
Print	Hotel and Motel Management			
Print	Household and Personal Products Industry			
Print	HR Focus			
Print	Human Relations			
Print	Inc.			
Print	Industrial and Corporate Change			
Print	Industrial and Labor Relations Review			
Print	Industry Week		W	
Print	INFOR: Information Systems and Operational Research			
Print	Information and Management			
Print	Journal of Business Ethics			
Print	Journal of Business Research			
Print	Journal of Consumer Research			
Print	Journal of Finance			
Print	Journal of International Business Studies			
Print	Journal of Management Information Systems			
Print	Journal of Marketing Research			
Print	Journal of Operations Management			
Print	Journal of Organizational Behavior			
Print	Journal of Retailing			
Print	Journal of World Business			
Print	Library Journal			
Print	Long Range Planning			
Print	Los Angeles Times			
Print	Management & Marketing			
Print	Management Science			
Print	Marketing			
Print	MIS Quarterly			
Print	MIT Sloan Management Review			
Print	Multinational Business Review			
Print	New York Times		W	
Print	Operations Research			
Print	Organizational Dynamics			
Print	Packaging Digest			
Print	Personnel Psychology			
Print	Platts			
Print	Progressive Grocer			
Print	Restaurant Business			
Print	Retail Merchandiser			
Print	Sales and Marketing Management			
Print	San Jose Mercury News		W	
Print	Searcher			

Type	Title	CBS MarketWatch: Keyword News Alert	Google News Alerts	YAHOO! Alerts
Print	Strategy and Leadership			
Print	Technology Review		W	
Print	Telephony			
Print	Textile World			
Print	Thunderbird International Business Review			
Print	Training			
Print	Travel Weekly			
Print	USA Today			
Print	Variety			
Print	Wall Street Journal			
Print	Washington Post			
Print	Wired Magazine			
Print	Women's Wear Daily		W	
Web	ATLANTA JOURNAL-CONSTITUTION (www.ajc.com)		X	
Web	BBC WORLD NEWS (news.bbc.co.uk)		X	
Web	BLOOMBERG (www.bloomberg.com)		X	
Web	BOSTON GLOBE (www.boston.com)		X	
Web	BUSINESS TIMES OF SINGAPORE (business-times.asia1.com.sg)		X	
Web	BUSINESS 2.0 (www.business2.com)			
Web	BUSINESSWEEK ONLINE (www.businessweek.com)		X	X
Web	BUSINESSWIRE (www.businesswire.com)	X		X
Web	CANADA NEWSWIRE (www.newswire.ca/en/)		(French version)	X
Web	CBC NEWS (www.cbc.ca)		X	
Web	CBS MARKETWATCH (cbs.marketwatch.com)	X	X	
Web	CFO (www.cfo.com)			
Web	CHICAGO SUN-TIMES (www.suntimes.com)		X	
Web	CHICAGO TRIBUNE (www.chicagotribune.com)		X	
Web	CHRISTIAN SCIENCE MONITOR (www.csmonitor.com)	X	X	
Web	CIO (www.cio.com)		X	
Web	CNBC (moneycentral.msn.com/investor/home.asp)			
Web	CNET (www.cnet.com)	X	X	
Web	CNN (www.cnn.com)		X	
Web	CNNFN (www.cnnfn.com)			
Web	CRAINS (www.crainsny.com)			
Web	C-SPAN (www.c-span.org)			
Web	DARWIN MAG (www.darwinmag.com)		X	
Web	ECONOMIST (www.economist.com)		X	
Web	FAST COMPANY (www.fastcompany.com)		X	
Web	FINANCIAL TIMES (www.ft.com)	X		X

Type	Title	CBS MarketWatch: Keyword News Alert	Google News Alerts	YAHOO! Alerts
Web	FORBES (www.forbes.com)		X	X
Web	FORTUNE (www.fortune.com)		X	
Web	FOX NEWS (www.foxnews.com)		X	
Web	GLOBE AND MAIL (www.globeandmail.com)		X	
Web	GUARDIAN (www.guardian.co.uk)		X	
Web	INTERNATIONAL HERALD TRIBUNE (www.iht.com)		X	
Web	INVESTOR'S BUSINESS DAILY (www.investors.com)		*	
Web	JOURNAL OF COMMERCE (www.joc.com)			
Web	KIPLINGER (www.kiplinger.com)			
Web	LA TIMES (www.latimes.com)			
Web	MIAMI HERALD (www.miami.com)		X	
Web	MIT TECH REVIEW (www.techreview.com)		X	
Web	MSN MONEY (moneycentral.msn.com/home.asp)		X	
Web	MSNBC (www.msnbc.com)		X	
Web	NEWSDAY (www.newsday.com)		X	
Web	NPR (www.npr.org)		X	
Web	NY POST (www.nypost.com)		X	
Web	NYTIMES (www.nytimes.com)		X	X
Web	PBS (www.pbs.org)		X	
Web	PR NEWSWIRE (www.prnewswire.com)	X	X	X
Web	RED HERRING (www.redherring.com)			
Web	REUTERS (www.reuters.com)		X	X
Web	SALON (www.salon.com)		*	
Web	SALT LAKE TRIBUNE (www.sltrib.com)		X	
Web	SAN JOSE MERCURY NEWS (www.mercurynews.com)		X	
Web	SEARCH ENGINE WATCH (www.searchenginewatch.com)		X	
Web	TECHNEWSWORLD (www.technewsworld.com)		*	
Web	TIMES ONLINE (www.timesonline.co.uk)		X	
Web	TORONTO STAR (www.thestar.com)		X	
Web	USA TODAY (www.usatoday.com)		X	X
Web	VENTUREWIRE (www.venturewire.com)			
Web	WASHINGTONPOST.COM (www.washingtonpost.com)		X	
Web	WIRED NEWS (www.wired.com)		X	
Web	WORLD PRESS REVIEW (www.worldpress.org)		X	
Web	YAHOO! NEWS (dailynews.yahoo.com)		X	
Web	ZDNET (www.zdnet.com)		X	

*Includes title, but site requires subscription

TABLE 2:
INEXPENSIVE NEWS ALERT SERVICES

- **New York Times News Tracker**
  (Not included in chart, as this service only covers the *New York Times.*)
- **Ft.com: News Alerts**
  (Not included in chart, as this service only covers the *Financial Times.*)
- **NetContent: IntelliSearch**
- **Highbean Research: eLibrary**
- **RocketInfo: RocketNews Enterprise**

Core Business Journal Title Coverage

Type	Title	NetContent IntelliSearch	HighBeam Research eLibrary*	RocketInfo: RocketNews Enterprise**
Print	Academy of Management Journal	P		
Print	Across the Board	P		W
Print	Administrative Science Quarterly	P		
Print	Advertising Age	W		W
Print	Adweek	W	P	W
Print	Air Conditioning, Heating & Refrigeration News			W
Print	American Banker	P		
Print	American Demographics	P	P	
Print	American Economic Review			
Print	Automotive News			W
Print	Aviation Week & Space Technology			W
Print	Barron's			W
Print	Bests Review			W
Print	Beverage Industry	P	P	W
Print	Beverage World	W	P	W
Print	Brandweek	W	P	W
Print	Broadcasting & Cable		P	W
Print	Business & Society			
Print	Business & Society Review			
Print	Business 2.0			
Print	Business Communication Quarterly		P	W
Print	Business Ethics Quarterly			
Print	Business History Review			
Print	Business Horizons			
Print	Business Week	W		
Print	California Management Review	P	P	
Print	Chain Store Age	P		W
Print	Chemical Marketing Reporter	P		
Print	Chemical Week	P	P	W
Print	Chicago Tribune	P		W
Print	Christian Science Monitor	W	P	W
Print	Dealerscope	P	P	W
Print	Decision Sciences	P		
Print	DSN Retailing			W
Print	Economist (U.K.)	P		W
Print	Electronic Business		P	W

Type	Title	NetContent IntelliSearch	HighBeam Research eLibrary*	RocketInfo: RocketNews Enterprise**
Print	ENR: Engineering News Record			W
Print	Euromoney	P		W
Print	Fast Company		P	W
Print	Financial Times (U.K.)			W
Print	Footwear News			W
Print	Forbes	W	P	W
Print	Fortune	P	P	W
Print	Guardian	P		
Print	Harvard Business Review		P	W
Print	Hotel and Motel Management	P, W	P	W
Print	Household and Personal Products Industry		P	W
Print	HR Focus	P	P	W
Print	Human Relations	P		W
Print	Inc.			W
Print	Industrial and Corporate Change			W
Print	Industrial and Labor Relations Review	P		W
Print	Industry Week	P	P	
Print	INFOR: Information Systems and Operational Research			
Print	Information and Management			
Print	Journal of Business Ethics			
Print	Journal of Business Research			
Print	Journal of Consumer Research			
Print	Journal of Finance			
Print	Journal of International Business Studies	P		
Print	Journal of Management Information Systems	P		
Print	Journal of Marketing Research	P		
Print	Journal of Operations Management			
Print	Journal of Organizational Behavior			
Print	Journal of Retailing			
Print	Journal of World Business			
Print	Library Journal		P	W
Print	Long Range Planning			
Print	Los Angeles Times			W
Print	Management & Marketing			W
Print	Management Science			
Print	Marketing	P		W
Print	MIS Quarterly	P		
Print	MIT Sloan Management Review		P	W
Print	Multinational Business Review	P		W
Print	New York Times	W		W
Print	Operations Research			
Print	Organizational Dynamics	P		
Print	Packaging Digest		P	W
Print	Personnel Psychology	P	P	
Print	Platts	W		W

Type	Title	NetContent IntelliSearch	HighBeam Research eLibrary*	RocketInfo: RocketNews Enterprise**
Print	Progressive Grocer	P		W
Print	Restaurant Business	P	P	W
Print	Retail Merchandiser		P	W
Print	Sales and Marketing Management	P	P	W
Print	San Jose Mercury News			
Print	Searcher		P	
Print	Strategy and Leadership	P		
Print	Technology Review		P	W
Print	Telephony	W	P	W
Print	Textile World	P	P	W
Print	Thunderbird International Business Review			
Print	Training	P		W
Print	Travel Weekly			W
Print	USA Today	W	P	W
Print	Variety		P	W
Print	Wall Street Journal			
Print	Washington Post	W	P	W
Print	Wired Magazine	W		W
Print	Women's Wear Daily			
Web	ATLANTA JOURNAL-CONSTITUTION (www.ajc.com)	X		X
Web	BBC WORLD NEWS (news.bbc.co.uk)	X		X
Web	BLOOMBERG (www.bloomberg.com)	X		X
Web	BOSTON GLOBE (www.boston.com)	X		X
Web	BUSINESS TIMES OF SINGAPORE (business-times.asia1.com.sg)			X
Web	BUSINESS 2.0 (www.business2.com)	X		X
Web	BUSINESSWEEK ONLINE (www.businessweek.com)	X		X
Web	BUSINESSWIRE (www.businesswire.com)	X		X
Web	CANADA NEWSWIRE (www.newswire.ca/en/)	X		X
Web	CBC NEWS (www.cbc.ca)	X		X
Web	CBS MARKETWATCH (cbs.marketwatch.com)	X		X
Web	CFO (www.cfo.com)	X		X
Web	CHICAGO SUN-TIMES (www.suntimes.com)	X		X
Web	CHICAGO TRIBUNE (www.chicagotribune.com)	X		X
Web	CHRISTIAN SCIENCE MONITOR (www.csmonitor.com)	X		X
Web	CIO (www.cio.com)	X		X
Web	CNBC (moneycentral.msn.com/investor/home.asp)	X		X
Web	CNET (www.cnet.com)	X		X
Web	CNN (www.cnn.com)	X		X

Type	Title	NetContent IntelliSearch	HighBeam Research eLibrary*	RocketInfo: RocketNews Enterprise**
Web	CNNFN (www.cnnfn.com)	X		X
Web	CRAINS (www.crainsny.com)			X
Web	C-SPAN (www.c-span.org)			
Web	DARWIN MAG (www.darwinmag.com)			X
Web	ECONOMIST (www.economist.com)	X		X
Web	FAST COMPANY (www.fastcompany.com)			X
Web	FINANCIAL TIMES (www.ft.com)	X		X
Web	FORBES (www.forbes.com)	X		X
Web	FORTUNE (www.fortune.com)	X		X
Web	FOX NEWS (www.foxnews.com)	X		X
Web	GLOBE AND MAIL (www.globeandmail.com)	X		X
Web	GUARDIAN (www.guardian.co.uk)	X		X
Web	INTERNATIONAL HERALD TRIBUNE (www.iht.com)	X		X
Web	INVESTOR'S BUSINESS DAILY (www.investors.com)			X
Web	JOURNAL OF COMMERCE (www.joc.com)	X		
Web	KIPLINGER (www.kiplinger.com)	X		X
Web	LA TIMES (www.latimes.com)			X
Web	MIAMI HERALD (www.miami.com)	X		X
Web	MIT TECH REVIEW (www.techreview.com)	X		X
Web	MSN MONEY (moneycentral.msn.com/home.asp)			X
Web	MSNBC (www.msnbc.com)	X		X
Web	NEWSDAY (www.newsday.com)	X		X
Web	NPR (www.npr.org)	X		X
Web	NY POST (www.nypost.com)	X		X
Web	NYTIMES (www.nytimes.com)	X		X
Web	PBS (www.pbs.org)			X
Web	PR NEWSWIRE (www.prnewswire.com)	X		X
Web	RED HERRING (www.redherring.com)			X
Web	REUTERS (www.reuters.com)	X		X
Web	SALON (www.salon.com)	X		X
Web	SALT LAKE TRIBUNE (www.sltrib.com)	X		X
Web	SAN JOSE MERCURY NEWS (www.mercurynews.com)	X		X
Web	SEARCH ENGINE WATCH (www.searchenginewatch.com)	X		X
Web	TECHNEWSWORLD (www.technewsworld.com)			X
Web	TIMES ONLINE (www.timesonline.co.uk)	X		X
Web	TORONTO STAR (www.thestar.com)	X		X
Web	USA TODAY (www.usatoday.com)	X		X
Web	VENTUREWIRE (www.venturewire.com)	X		
Web	WASHINGTONPOST.COM (www.washingtonpost.com)	X		X

Type	Title	NetContent IntelliSearch	HighBeam Research eLibrary*	RocketInfo: RocketNews Enterprise**
Web	WIRED NEWS (www.wired.com)	X		X
Web	WORLD PRESS REVIEW (www.worldpress.org)			
Web	YAHOO! NEWS (dailynews.yahoo.com)			
Web	ZDNET (www.zdnet.com)			

TABLE 3A:
FEE-BASED/PREMIUM NEWS ALERT SERVICES

- **Burrelle's/Luce: NewsAlert**
  (Not included in chart, as the vendor did not want to release its source list.)
- **CustomScoop and FNS: NewsClips Online**
  (FNS has the same textual source coverage as CustomScoop, though FNS adds several radio and television broadcast Web sites.)
- **CyberAlert**
- **Dialog: NewsEdge and Hoover's News Alerts**
  (In-depth business, industry, trade sources.)

Core Business Journal Title Coverage

Type	Title	CustomScoop (and FNS)	CyberAlert	Dialog: NewsEdge (and Hoover's News Alerts)
Print	Academy of Management Journal			
Print	Across the Board		W	
Print	Administrative Science Quarterly			
Print	Advertising Age	W	W	P
Print	Adweek	W	W	
Print	Air Conditioning, Heating & Refrigeration News	W	W	
Print	American Banker	W	W	P
Print	American Demographics		W	
Print	American Economic Review			
Print	Automotive News	W	W	P
Print	Aviation Week & Space Technology	W	W	
Print	Barron's		W	
Print	Bests Review		W	P
Print	Beverage Industry			P
Print	Beverage World	W	W	
Print	Brandweek	W	W	P
Print	Broadcasting & Cable	W	W	
Print	Business & Society			
Print	Business & Society Review			
Print	Business 2.0	W	W	
Print	Business Communication Quarterly			
Print	Business Ethics Quarterly			
Print	Business History Review			
Print	Business Horizons		W	

Type	Title	CustomScoop (and FNS)	CyberAlert	Dialog: NewsEdge (and Hoover's News Alerts)
Print	Business Week	W	W	P
Print	California Management Review			
Print	Chain Store Age	W	W	P
Print	Chemical Marketing Reporter			P
Print	Chemical Week		W	P
Print	Chicago Tribune	W	W	P
Print	Christian Science Monitor	W	W	
Print	Dealerscope	W	W	
Print	Decision Sciences			
Print	DSN Retailing	W	W	
Print	Economist (U.K.)	W	W	P
Print	Electronic Business	W	W	P
Print	ENR: Engineering News Record	W	W	
Print	Euromoney		W	
Print	Fast Company	W	W	
Print	Financial Times (U.K.)	W	W	P
Print	Footwear News	W	W	
Print	Forbes	W	W	P
Print	Fortune	W	W	P
Print	Guardian	W	W	
Print	Harvard Business Review		W	
Print	Hotel and Motel Management	W	W	
Print	Household and Personal Products Industry		W	
Print	HR Focus			
Print	Human Relations		W	
Print	Inc.		W	
Print	Industrial and Corporate Change			
Print	Industrial and Labor Relations Review			
Print	Industry Week	W	W	P
Print	INFOR: Information Systems and Operational Research			
Print	Information and Management			
Print	Journal of Business Ethics			
Print	Journal of Business Research			
Print	Journal of Consumer Research			
Print	Journal of Finance			
Print	Journal of International Business Studies			
Print	Journal of Management Information Systems		W	
Print	Journal of Marketing Research			
Print	Journal of Operations Management			
Print	Journal of Organizational Behavior			
Print	Journal of Retailing			P
Print	Journal of World Business			
Print	Library Journal		W	P
Print	Long Range Planning			

Type	Title	CustomScoop (and FNS)	CyberAlert	Dialog: NewsEdge (and Hoover's News Alerts)
Print	Los Angeles Times	W	W	P
Print	Management & Marketing		W	
Print	Management Science		W	
Print	Marketing		W	P
Print	MIS Quarterly		W	
Print	MIT Sloan Management Review	W		
Print	Multinational Business Review			
Print	New York Times	W	W	P
Print	Operations Research			
Print	Organizational Dynamics			
Print	Packaging Digest	W	W	
Print	Personnel Psychology		W	
Print	Platts	W	W	P
Print	Progressive Grocer	W	W	P
Print	Restaurant Business	W	W	
Print	Retail Merchandiser	W	W	
Print	Sales and Marketing Management		W	
Print	San Jose Mercury News	W	W	P
Print	Searcher		W	
Print	Strategy and Leadership			
Print	Technology Review	W	W	P
Print	Telephony	W	W	P
Print	Textile World	W	W	
Print	Thunderbird International Business Review		W	
Print	Training		W	
Print	Travel Weekly	W	W	
Print	USA Today	W	W	P
Print	Variety	W		P
Print	Wall Street Journal			P
Print	Washington Post	W	W	P
Print	Wired Magazine	W	W	
Print	Women's Wear Daily		W	
Web	ATLANTA JOURNAL-CONSTITUTION (www.ajc.com)	X	X	DF
Web	BBC WORLD NEWS (news.bbc.co.uk)	X	X	
Web	BLOOMBERG (www.bloomberg.com)	X	X	DF
Web	BOSTON GLOBE (www.boston.com)	X	X	DF
Web	BUSINESS TIMES OF SINGAPORE (business-times.asia1.com.sg)	X	X	
Web	BUSINESS 2.0 (www.business2.com)	X	X	
Web	BUSINESSWEEK ONLINE (www.businessweek.com)	X	X	DF
Web	BUSINESSWIRE (www.businesswire.com)	X	X	DF
Web	CANADA NEWSWIRE (www.newswire.ca/en/)	X	X	DF
Web	CBC NEWS (www.cbc.ca)	X	X	
Web	CBS MARKETWATCH (cbs.marketwatch.com)	X	X	DF

Type	Title	CustomScoop (and FNS)	CyberAlert	Dialog: NewsEdge (and Hoover's News Alerts)
Web	CFO (www.cfo.com)	X	X	
Web	CHICAGO SUN-TIMES (www.suntimes.com)	X	X	DF
Web	CHICAGO TRIBUNE (www.chicagotribune.com)	X	X	DF
Web	CHRISTIAN SCIENCE MONITOR (www.csmonitor.com)	X	X	
Web	CIO (www.cio.com)	X	X	
Web	CNBC (moneycentral.msn.com /investor/home.asp)	X	X	
Web	CNET (www.cnet.com)	X	X	DF
Web	CNN (www.cnn.com)	X	X	
Web	CNNFN (www.cnnfn.com)	X	X	
Web	CRAINS (www.crainsny.com)	X	X	
Web	C-SPAN (www.c-span.org)	X	X	
Web	DARWIN MAG (www.darwinmag.com)	X	X	
Web	ECONOMIST (www.economist.com)	X	X	DF
Web	FAST COMPANY (www.fastcompany.com)	X	X	DF
Web	FINANCIAL TIMES (www.ft.com)	X	X	DF
Web	FORBES (www.forbes.com)	X	X	DF
Web	FORTUNE (www.fortune.com)	X	X	
Web	FOX NEWS (www.foxnews.com)	X	X	
Web	GLOBE AND MAIL (www.globeandmail.com)	X	X	DF
Web	GUARDIAN (www.guardian.co.uk)	X	X	
Web	INTERNATIONAL HERALD TRIBUNE (www.iht.com)	X	X	DF
Web	INVESTOR'S BUSINESS DAILY (www.investors.com)	X	X	
Web	JOURNAL OF COMMERCE (www.joc.com)	X	X	
Web	KIPLINGER (www.kiplinger.com)	X	X	DF
Web	LA TIMES (www.latimes.com)	X	X	DF
Web	MIAMI HERALD (www.miami.com)	X	X	DF
Web	MIT TECH REVIEW (www.techreview.com)	X	X	DF
Web	MSN MONEY (moneycentral.msn.com/home.asp)	X	X	
Web	MSNBC (www.msnbc.com)	X	X	
Web	NEWSDAY (www.newsday.com)	X	X	
Web	NPR (www.npr.org)	X	X	
Web	NY POST (www.nypost.com)	X	X	
Web	NYTIMES (www.nytimes.com)	X	X	DF
Web	PBS (www.pbs.org)	X	X	
Web	PR NEWSWIRE (www.prnewswire.com)	X	X	DF
Web	RED HERRING (www.redherring.com)	X	X	
Web	REUTERS (www.reuters.com)	X	X	DF

Type	Title	CustomScoop (and FNS)	CyberAlert	Dialog: NewsEdge (and Hoover's News Alerts)
Web	SALON (www.salon.com)	X	X	
Web	SALT LAKE TRIBUNE (www.sltrib.com)	X	X	DF
Web	SAN JOSE MERCURY NEWS (www.mercurynews.com)	X	X	DF
Web	SEARCH ENGINE WATCH (www.searchenginewatch.com)	X	X	
Web	TECHNEWSWORLD (www.technewsworld.com)	X	X	
Web	TIMES ONLINE (www.timesonline.co.uk)	X	X	
Web	TORONTO STAR (www.thestar.com)	X	X	DF
Web	USA TODAY (www.usatoday.com)	X	X	
Web	VENTUREWIRE (www.venturewire.com)	X	X	
Web	WASHINGTONPOST.COM (www.washingtonpost.com)	X	X	DF
Web	WIRED NEWS (www.wired.com)	X	X	
Web	WORLD PRESS REVIEW (www.worldpress.org)	X	X	DF
Web	YAHOO! NEWS (dailynews.yahoo.com)	X	X	
Web	ZDNET (www.zdnet.com)	X	X	DF

TABLE 3B:
FEE-BASED/PREMIUM NEWS ALERT SERVICES

- **FT.Com: Global Media Monitor**
  (Note that while this service does not include too many of these U.S.-based business news sources, it does offer an excellent content collection of non-Western, global daily newspapers, and information sources.)
- **Moreover: CI Alerts**
- **Nexcerpt**
- **PR Newswire: eWatch**

Core Business Journal Title Coverage

Type	Title	FT.COM Global Media	Moreover ci-alerts	Nexcerpt	PR Newswire eWatch
Print	Academy of Management Journal				
Print	Across the Board			W	
Print	Administrative Science Quarterly			W	
Print	Advertising Age		W	W	W

Type	Title	FT.COM Global Media	Moreover ci-alerts	Nexcerpt	PR Newswire eWatch
Print	Adweek		W	W	W
Print	Air Conditioning, Heating & Refrigeration News		W		W
Print	American Banker		W		W
Print	American Demographics				W
Print	American Economic Review				
Print	Automotive News		W	W	W
Print	Aviation Week & Space Technology		W	W	W
Print	Barron's		W		W
Print	Bests Review	P	W		
Print	Beverage Industry				W
Print	Beverage World				W
Print	Brandweek		W	W	W
Print	Broadcasting & Cable		W		W
Print	Business & Society				
Print	Business & Society Review				
Print	Business 2.0		W	W	
Print	Business Communication Quarterly				
Print	Business Ethics Quarterly			W	
Print	Business History Review			W	
Print	Business Horizons				
Print	Business Week	P	W	W	W
Print	California Management Review				
Print	Chain Store Age		W	W	W
Print	Chemical Marketing Reporter		W		
Print	Chemical Week		W		
Print	Chicago Tribune		W	W	W
Print	Christian Science Monitor		W	W	W
Print	Dealerscope			W	W
Print	Decision Sciences				
Print	DSN Retailing				W
Print	Economist (U.K.)	P	W	W	W
Print	Electronic Business		W		W
Print	ENR: Engineering News Record		W		W
Print	Euromoney		W		
Print	Fast Company		W	W	W
Print	Financial Times (U.K.)	P	W	W	W
Print	Footwear News				W
Print	Forbes		W	W	W
Print	Fortune		W	W	W
Print	Guardian		W	W	
Print	Harvard Business Review		W		W
Print	Hotel and Motel Management		W		W
Print	Household and Personal Products Industry				W
Print	HR Focus				
Print	Human Relations				
Print	Inc.		W	W	W
Print	Industrial and Corporate Change		W		

Type	Title	FT.COM Global Media	Moreover ci-alerts	Nexcerpt	PR Newswire eWatch
Print	Industrial and Labor Relations Review				
Print	Industry Week		W	W	W
Print	INFOR: Information Systems and Operational Research			W	
Print	Information and Management			W	
Print	Journal of Business Ethics			W	
Print	Journal of Business Research				
Print	Journal of Consumer Research				
Print	Journal of Finance				
Print	Journal of International Business Studies				
Print	Journal of Management Information Systems				
Print	Journal of Marketing Research				
Print	Journal of Operations Management				
Print	Journal of Organizational Behavior				
Print	Journal of Retailing				
Print	Journal of World Business				
Print	Library Journal		W		
Print	Long Range Planning				
Print	Los Angeles Times		W	W	W
Print	Management & Marketing				W
Print	Management Science				
Print	Marketing	P			W
Print	MIS Quarterly				
Print	MIT Sloan Management Review		W		
Print	Multinational Business Review				
Print	New York Times		W	W	W
Print	Operations Research				
Print	Organizational Dynamics				
Print	Packaging Digest		W		W
Print	Personnel Psychology				
Print	Platts		W	W	W
Print	Progressive Grocer		W	W	W
Print	Restaurant Business		W		W
Print	Retail Merchandiser		W		W
Print	Sales and Marketing Management		W		W
Print	San Jose Mercury News		W	W	W
Print	Searcher			W	
Print	Strategy and Leadership				
Print	Technology Review		W	W	W
Print	Telephony			W	W
Print	Textile World		W		W
Print	Thunderbird International Business Review				
Print	Training		W		
Print	Travel Weekly		W		

Type	Title	FT.COM Global Media	Moreover ci-alerts	Nexcerpt	PR Newswire eWatch
Print	USA Today		W	W	W
Print	Variety		W	W	W
Print	Wall Street Journal	P	W		W
Print	Washington Post	P	W	W	W
Print	Wired Magazine		W	W	W
Print	Women's Wear Daily		W		W
Web	ATLANTA JOURNAL-CONSTITUTION (www.ajc.com)		X	X	X
Web	BBC WORLD NEWS (news.bbc.co.uk)	DF	X	X	X
Web	BLOOMBERG (www.bloomberg.com)		X	X	X
Web	BOSTON GLOBE (www.boston.com)		X	X	X
Web	BUSINESS TIMES OF SINGAPORE (business-times.asia1.com.sg)		X	X	X
Web	BUSINESS 2.0 (www.business2.com)		X	X	X
Web	BUSINESSWEEK ONLINE (www.businessweek.com)		X	X	X
Web	BUSINESSWIRE (www.businesswire.com)		X	X	X
Web	CANADA NEWSWIRE (www.newswire.ca/en/)	DF	X	X	X
Web	CBC NEWS (www.cbc.ca)		X	X	X
Web	CBS MARKETWATCH (cbs.marketwatch.com)	DF	X	X	X
Web	CFO (www.cfo.com)		X		X
Web	CHICAGO SUN-TIMES (www.suntimes.com)		X	X	X
Web	CHICAGO TRIBUNE (www.chicagotribune.com)		X		X
Web	CHRISTIAN SCIENCE MONITOR (www.csmonitor.com)		X	X	X
Web	CIO (www.cio.com)		X	X	X
Web	CNBC (moneycentral.msn.com/investor/home.asp)	DF	X	X	X
Web	CNET (www.cnet.com)		X	X	X
Web	CNN (www.cnn.com)		X	X	X
Web	CNNFN (www.cnnfn.com)	DF	X	X	X
Web	CRAINS (www.crainsny.com)		X	X	X
Web	C-SPAN (www.c-span.org)		X		
Web	DARWIN MAG (www.darwinmag.com)		X		X
Web	ECONOMIST (www.economist.com)	DF	X	X	X
Web	FAST COMPANY (www.fastcompany.com)		X	X	X
Web	FINANCIAL TIMES (www.ft.com)	DF	X	X	X

Type	Title	FT.COM Global Media	Moreover ci-alerts	Nexcerpt	PR Newswire eWatch
Web	FORBES (www.forbes.com)		X	X	
Web	FORTUNE (www.fortune.com)		X	X	X
Web	FOX NEWS (www.foxnews.com)	DF	X	X	X
Web	GLOBE AND MAIL (www.globeandmail.com)		X	X	X
Web	GUARDIAN (www.guardian.co.uk)	DF	X	X	X
Web	INTERNATIONAL HERALD TRIBUNE (www.iht.com)	DF	X	X	X
Web	INVESTOR'S BUSINESS DAILY (www.investors.com)		X		X
Web	JOURNAL OF COMMERCE (www.joc.com)		X	X	X
Web	KIPLINGER (www.kiplinger.com)		X	X	X
Web	LA TIMES (www.latimes.com)		X	X	X
Web	MIAMI HERALD (www.miami.com)		X	X	X
Web	MIT TECH REVIEW (www.techreview.com)		X	X	X
Web	MSN MONEY (moneycentral.msn.com/home.asp)		X	X	X
Web	MSNBC (www.msnbc.com)	DF	X	X	X
Web	NEWSDAY (www.newsday.com)		X	X	X
Web	NPR (www.npr.org)		X	X	X
Web	NY POST (www.nypost.com)		X	X	X
Web	NYTIMES (www.nytimes.com)		X	X	X
Web	PBS (www.pbs.org)		X		X
Web	PR NEWSWIRE (www.prnewswire.com)		X	X	X
Web	RED HERRING (www.redherring.com)		X	X	X
Web	REUTERS (www.reuters.com)		X	X	X
Web	SALON (www.salon.com)		X	X	X
Web	SALT LAKE TRIBUNE (www.sltrib.com)		X	X	X
Web	SAN JOSE MERCURY NEWS (www.mercurynews.com)		X	X	X
Web	SEARCH ENGINE WATCH (www.searchenginewatch.com)		X	X	X
Web	TECHNEWSWORLD (www.technewsworld.com)		X		X
Web	TIMES ONLINE (www.timesonline.co.uk)		X		X
Web	TORONTO STAR (www.thestar.com)		X	X	X

Type	Title	FT.COM Global Media	Moreover ci-alerts	Nexcerpt	PR Newswire eWatch
Web	USA TODAY (www.usatoday.com)		X	X	X
Web	VENTUREWIRE (www.venturewire.com)		X		X
Web	WASHINGTONPOST.COM (www.washingtonpost.com)	DF	X	X	X
Web	WIRED NEWS (www.wired.com)		X	X	X
Web	WORLD PRESS REVIEW (www.worldpress.org)		X	X	
Web	YAHOO! NEWS (dailynews.yahoo.com)		X	X	X
Web	ZDNET (www.zdnet.com)		X	X	X

TABLE 3C:
FEE-BASED/PREMIUM NEWS ALERT SERVICES

- **Yellowbrix**
- **WebClipping.com**

Core Business Journal Title Coverage

Type	Title	YellowBrix	WebClipping
Print	Academy of Management Journal		W
Print	Across the Board	P	
Print	Administrative Science Quarterly		
Print	Advertising Age	P	W
Print	Adweek		W
Print	Air Conditioning, Heating & Refrigeration News		
Print	American Banker	P	W
Print	American Demographics	P	W
Print	American Economic Review	P	
Print	Automotive News		
Print	Aviation Week & Space Technology		
Print	Barron's		
Print	Bests Review	P	W
Print	Beverage Industry	P	W
Print	Beverage World		
Print	Brandweek		W
Print	Broadcasting & Cable	P	
Print	Business & Society		
Print	Business & Society Review		
Print	Business 2.0		W
Print	Business Communication Quarterly	P	
Print	Business Ethics Quarterly		
Print	Business History Review		
Print	Business Horizons		
Print	Business Week	P	
Print	California Management Review		

Type	Title	YellowBrix	WebClipping
Print	Chain Store Age		W
Print	Chemical Marketing Reporter	P	
Print	Chemical Week	P	
Print	Chicago Tribune	P	W
Print	Christian Science Monitor	P	W
Print	Dealerscope	P	
Print	Decision Sciences	P	
Print	DSN Retailing		W
Print	Economist (U.K.)	P	W
Print	Electronic Business	P	
Print	ENR: Engineering News Record		
Print	Euromoney	P	
Print	Fast Company		
Print	Financial Times (U.K.)		W
Print	Footwear News		
Print	Forbes	P	(Forbes ASAP) W
Print	Fortune	P	W
Print	Guardian	P	W
Print	Harvard Business Review		
Print	Hotel and Motel Management		
Print	Household and Personal Products Industry		
Print	HR Focus	P	
Print	Human Relations		
Print	Inc.		
Print	Industrial and Corporate Change		
Print	Industrial and Labor Relations Review	P	
Print	Industry Week	P	W
Print	INFOR: Information Systems and Operational Research	P	
Print	Information and Management	P	
Print	Journal of Business Ethics	P	
Print	Journal of Business Research	P	
Print	Journal of Consumer Research	P	
Print	Journal of Finance	P	
Print	Journal of International Business Studies	P	
Print	Journal of Management Information Systems	P	
Print	Journal of Marketing Research	P	
Print	Journal of Operations Management		
Print	Journal of Organizational Behavior		
Print	Journal of Retailing		
Print	Journal of World Business		
Print	Library Journal	P	W
Print	Long Range Planning		
Print	Los Angeles Times	P	
Print	Management & Marketing	P	
Print	Management Science	P	
Print	Marketing	P	CF
Print	MIS Quarterly	P	
Print	MIT Sloan Management Review		W
Print	Multinational Business Review	P	
Print	New York Times		"News Services" W

Type	Title	YellowBrix	WebClipping
Print	Operations Research		
Print	Organizational Dynamics	P	
Print	Packaging Digest	P	
Print	Personnel Psychology	P	
Print	Platts		
Print	Progressive Grocer		W
Print	Restaurant Business	P	W
Print	Retail Merchandiser	P	
Print	Sales and Marketing Management		
Print	San Jose Mercury News	P	W
Print	Searcher	P	
Print	Strategy and Leadership		
Print	Technology Review	P	
Print	Telephony	P	W
Print	Textile World	P	
Print	Thunderbird International Business Review		
Print	Training	P	
Print	Travel Weekly	P	W
Print	USA Today	P	W
Print	Variety	P	
Print	Wall Street Journal	P	(Classroom edition) W
Print	Washington Post	P	W
Print	Wired Magazine		W
Print	Women's Wear Daily		
Web	ATLANTA JOURNAL-CONSTITUTION (www.ajc.com)	DF	X
Web	BBC WORLD NEWS (news.bbc.co.uk)	DF	
Web	BLOOMBERG (www.bloomberg.com)		X
Web	BOSTON GLOBE (www.boston.com)	DF	
Web	BUSINESS TIMES OF SINGAPORE (business-times.asia1.com.sg)	DF	
Web	BUSINESS 2.0 (www.business2.com)		X
Web	BUSINESSWEEK ONLINE (www.businessweek.com)	DF	
Web	BUSINESSWIRE (www.businesswire.com)	DF	X
Web	CANADA NEWSWIRE (www.newswire.ca/en/)	DF	X
Web	CBC NEWS (www.cbc.ca)		
Web	CBS MARKETWATCH (cbs.marketwatch.com)		X
Web	CFO (www.cfo.com)		
Web	CHICAGO SUN-TIMES (www.suntimes.com)	DF	X
Web	CHICAGO TRIBUNE (www.chicagotribune.com)	DF	X
Web	CHRISTIAN SCIENCE MONITOR (www.csmonitor.com)	DF	X
Web	CIO (www.cio.com)		X
Web	CNBC (moneycentral.msn.com/investor/home.asp)		X
Web	CNET (www.cnet.com)	DF	X
Web	CNN (www.cnn.com)		X
Web	CNNFN (www.cnnfn.com)		X
Web	CRAINS (www.crainsny.com)	DF	X
Web	C-SPAN (www.c-span.org)		
Web	DARWIN MAG (www.darwinmag.com)		X
Web	ECONOMIST (www.economist.com)	DF	X

Type	Title	YellowBrix	WebClipping
Web	FAST COMPANY (www.fastcompany.com)		
Web	FINANCIAL TIMES (www.ft.com)	DF	X
Web	FORBES (www.forbes.com)	DF	(Forbes ASAP) X
Web	FORTUNE (www.fortune.com)	DF	X
Web	FOX NEWS (www.foxnews.com)		X
Web	GLOBE AND MAIL (www.globeandmail.com)	DF	X
Web	GUARDIAN (www.guardian.co.uk)	DF	X
Web	INTERNATIONAL HERALD TRIBUNE (www.iht.com)	DF	
Web	INVESTOR'S BUSINESS DAILY (www.investors.com)		
Web	JOURNAL OF COMMERCE (www.joc.com)		
Web	KIPLINGER (www.kiplinger.com)		
Web	LA TIMES (www.latimes.com)	DF	X
Web	MIAMI HERALD (www.miami.com)	DF	X
Web	MIT TECH REVIEW (www.techreview.com)	DF	
Web	MSN MONEY (moneycentral.msn.com/home.asp)		
Web	MSNBC (www.msnbc.com)		X
Web	NEWSDAY (www.newsday.com)	DF	
Web	NPR (www.npr.org)		
Web	NY POST (www.nypost.com)		X
Web	NYTIMES (www.nytimes.com)		(News Services) X
Web	PBS (www.pbs.org)		
Web	PR NEWSWIRE (www.prnewswire.com)		
Web	RED HERRING (www.redherring.com)		
Web	REUTERS (www.reuters.com)		
Web	SALON (www.salon.com)		X
Web	SALT LAKE TRIBUNE (www.sltrib.com)	DF	X
Web	SAN JOSE MERCURY NEWS (www.mercurynews.com)	DF	X
Web	SEARCH ENGINE WATCH (www.searchenginewatch.com)		
Web	TECHNEWSWORLD (www.technewsworld.com)	DF	X
Web	TIMES ONLINE (www.timesonline.co.uk)		
Web	TORONTO STAR (www.thestar.com)		X
Web	USA TODAY (www.usatoday.com)	DF	X
Web	VENTUREWIRE (www.venturewire.com)	DF	X
Web	WASHINGTONPOST.COM (www.washingtonpost.com)	DF	X
Web	WIRED NEWS (www.wired.com)		X
Web	WORLD PRESS REVIEW (www.worldpress.org)	DF	X
Web	YAHOO! NEWS (dailynews.yahoo.com)		X
Web	ZDNET (www.zdnet.com)		X

TABLE: 4
TRADITIONAL ONLINE NEWS ALERT VENDORS

- **Dialog: Newsroom**
  (To look up sources, link to www.dialog.com/sources/newsroom/.)
- **Factive: Track Module**
  (To look up sources, link to www.factiva.com/sources/search.asp?node=menu Elem1523.)
- **Intelligence Data: Insite 2**
- **LexisNexis: Personal News**
  (To look up sources, link to web.nexis.com/sources/.)

Core Business Journal Coverage

Type	Title	Dialog: NewsRoom	Factiva: Track	Intelligance Data: InSite 2	LexisNexis Personal News*
Print	Academy of Management Journal	P	(Abstracts) P	P	P
Print	Across the Board	P	P	(Summary) P	P
Print	Administrative Science Quarterly	P	(Abstracts) P	P	P
Print	Advertising Age	P	P	P	P
Print	Adweek	P	P	P	P
Print	Air Conditioning, Heating & Refrigeration News	P	P	P	P
Print	American Banker	P	P	P	P
Print	American Demographics	(Abstracts) P	P	P	P
Print	American Economic Review			(Summary) P	(Abstracts) P
Print	Automotive News	P	P	P	P
Print	Aviation Week & Space Technology	P	P	P	P
Print	Barron's	(Abstracts) P	P	(Summary) P	(Abstracts) P
Print	Bests Review	P	P	P	P
Print	Beverage Industry	P	P	P	P
Print	Beverage World	P	P	P	P
Print	Brandweek	P	P	P	P
Print	Broadcasting & Cable	P	P	P	P
Print	Business & Society	P	P	P	P
Print	Business & Society Review		(Abstracts) P	(Summary) P	
Print	Business 2.0				(Abstracts) P
Print	Business Communication Quarterly	P	P		P
Print	Business Ethics Quarterly	(Abstracts) P	(Abstracts) P		(Abstracts) P
Print	Business History Review	P			P

Type	Title	Dialog: NewsRoom	Factiva: Track	Intelligance Data: InSite 2	LexisNexis Personal News*
Print	Business Horizons			P	(Abstracts) P
Print	Business Week	P	P	P	P
Print	California Management Review	P		P	P
Print	Chain Store Age	(Abstracts) P	P	(Summary) P	P
Print	Chemical Marketing Reporter	(Abstracts) P	P	(Summary) P	P
Print	Chemical Week	P	P	P	P
Print	Chicago Tribune		P	P	P
Print	Christian Science Monitor	P	P		P
Print	Dealerscope	(Abstracts) P	P		P
Print	Decision Sciences	P	P	(Summary) P	(Abstracts) P
Print	DSN Retailing	P	P	P	P
Print	Economist (U.K.)	P		(Summary) P	P
Print	Electronic Business	P	P	P	P
Print	ENR: Engineering News Record	P	P	(Summary) P	P
Print	Euromoney	(Abstracts) P	P	(Summary) P	P
Print	Fast Company	(Abstracts) P	P	(Summary) P	P
Print	Financial Times (U.K.)	P	P		P
Print	Footwear News	P	P	P	P
Print	Forbes	P	P	P	P
Print	Fortune	(Abstracts) P	P	P	P
Print	Guardian	P	P	(Summary) P	P
Print	Harvard Business Review	P	P	(Summary) P	P
Print	Hotel and Motel Management	(Abstracts) P	P	P	P
Print	Household and Personal Products Industry	P	P	P	P
Print	HR Focus	P	P	P	P
Print	Human Relations	P	P	(Summary) P	P
Print	Inc.	(Abstracts) P		P	P
Print	Industrial and Corporate Change				P
Print	Industrial and Labor Relations Review	P	(Abstracts) P	P	P
Print	Industry Week	P	P	P	P

Type	Title	Dialog: NewsRoom	Factiva: Track	Intelligance Data: InSite 2	LexisNexis Personal News*
Print	INFOR: Information Systems and Operational Research				P
Print	Information and Management	(Abstracts) P		(Summary) P	(Abstracts) P
Print	Journal of Business Ethics	(Abstracts) P	(Abstracts) P	(Summary) P	P
Print	Journal of Business Research	(Abstracts) P	(Abstracts) P	(Summary) P	P
Print	Journal of Consumer Research			P	P
Print	Journal of Finance	P		P	(Abstracts) P
Print	Journal of International Business Studies	P		P	P
Print	Journal of Management Information Systems	(Abstracts) P			P
Print	Journal of Marketing Research			(Summary) P	P
Print	Journal of Operations Management	P		(Summary) P	P
Print	Journal of Organizational Behavior			(Summary) P	(Abstracts) P
Print	Journal of Retailing			P	P
Print	Journal of World Business	(Abstracts) P		P	P
Print	Library Journal	P	P	P	P
Print	Long Range Planning		(Abstracts) P	(Summary) P	P
Print	Los Angeles Times				P
Print	Management & Marketing			(Summary) P	
Print	Management Science			(Summary) P	(Abstracts) P
Print	Marketing	P	P	P	P
Print	MIS Quarterly	P	P	P	P
Print	MIT Sloan Management Review	(Abstracts)		P	(Abstracts) P
Print	Multinational Business Review	P	P		
Print	New York Times	P	P	(Summary) P	
Print	Operations Research	(Abstracts) P		(Summary) P	(Abstracts) P
Print	Organizational Dynamics	(Abstracts) P		P	P
Print	Packaging Digest	P		P	P
Print	Personnel Psychology	P	P	P	P

Type	Title	Dialog: NewsRoom	Factiva: Track	Intelligance Data: InSite 2	LexisNexis Personal News*
Print	Platts	P	P	(Summary) P	P
Print	Progressive Grocer	P	P	P	P
Print	Restaurant Business	P	P	P	P
Print	Retail Merchandiser	P	P	P	P
Print	Sales and Marketing Management	P	P	P	P
Print	San Jose Mercury News	P	P	(Summary) P	P
Print	Searcher	P		P	P
Print	Strategy and Leadership	P		(Summary) P	P
Print	Technology Review	P	P	P	P
Print	Telephony	P	P	P	P
Print	Textile World	P		P	P
Print	Thunderbird International Business Review	(Abstracts) P			P
Print	Training	(Abstracts) P	P	P	P
Print	Travel Weekly	P	P	P	P
Print	USA Today	P	P	(Summary) P	P
Print	Variety	P	P	P	P
Print	Wall Street Journal	(Abstracts) P	P	(Summary) Europe Ed.	(Abstracts) P
Print	Washington Post		P		P
Print	Wired Magazine	(Abstracts) P			
Print	Women's Wear Daily	P	P		P
Web	ATLANTA JOURNAL-CONSTITUTION (www.ajc.com)	DF	DF		DF
Web	BBC WORLD NEWS (news.bbc.co.uk)	DF	DF		(World Monitoring) DF
Web	BLOOMBERG (www.bloomberg.com)	DF			DF
Web	BOSTON GLOBE (www.boston.com)	DF	DF	DF	DF
Web	BUSINESS TIMES OF SINGAPORE (business-times.asia1.com.sg)	DF	DF	DF	DF
Web	BUSINESS 2.0 (www.business2.com)				(Abstracts) DF
Web	BUSINESSWEEK ONLINE (www.businessweek.com)		DF	DF	DF
Web	BUSINESSWIRE (www.businesswire.com)	DF	DF		DF

Type	Title	Dialog: NewsRoom	Factiva: Track	Intelligance Data: InSite 2	LexisNexis Personal News*
Web	CANADA NEWSWIRE (www.newswire.ca/en/)	DF	DF		DF
Web	CBC NEWS (www.cbc.ca)		DF		
Web	CBS MARKETWATCH (cbs.marketwatch.com)	DF	DF		DF
Web	CFO (www.cfo.com)	(Abstracts) DF	DF	DF	DF
Web	CHICAGO SUN-TIMES (www.suntimes.com)	DF	DF	DF	DF
Web	CHICAGO TRIBUNE (www.chicagotribune.com)		DF	DF	DF
Web	CHRISTIAN SCIENCE MONITOR (www.csmonitor.com)	DF	DF		DF
Web	CIO (www.cio.com)	(Abstracts) DF		(Summary) DF	DF
Web	CNBC (moneycentral.msn.com/ investor/home.asp)		DF		DF
Web	CNET (www.cnet.com)		DF		
Web	CNN (www.cnn.com)	DF	DF		DF
Web	CNNFN (www.cnnfn.com)	DF	DF		DF
Web	CRAINS (www.crainsny.com)	DF			DF
Web	C-SPAN (www.c-span.org)				(Abstracts) DF
Web	DARWIN MAG (www.darwinmag.com)				
Web	ECONOMIST (www.economist.com)	DF	DF	DF	DF
Web	FAST COMPANY (www.fastcompany.com)	(Abstracts) DF	DF	DF	DF
Web	FINANCIAL TIMES (www.ft.com)	DF	DF	DF	DF
Web	FORBES (www.forbes.com)	DF	DF	DF	DF
Web	FORTUNE (www.fortune.com)	(Abstracts)	DF	DF	DF
Web	FOX NEWS (www.foxnews.com)		DF		DF
Web	GLOBE AND MAIL (www.globeandmail.com)	(Abstracts) DF	DF	DF	DF
Web	GUARDIAN (www.guardian.co.uk)	DF	DF	DF	DF
Web	INTERNATIONAL HERALD TRIBUNE (www.iht.com)	DF	DF		DF
Web	INVESTOR'S BUSINESS DAILY (www.investors.com)		DF		DF
Web	JOURNAL OF COMMERCE (www.joc.com)		DF	DF	DF

Type	Title	Dialog: NewsRoom	Factiva: Track	Intelligance Data: InSite 2	LexisNexis Personal News*
Web	KIPLINGER (www.kiplinger.com)	DF	DF	DF	DF
Web	LA TIMES (www.latimes.com)		DF	DF	DF
Web	MIAMI HERALD (www.miami.com)	DF	DF	DF	DF
Web	MIT TECH REVIEW (www.techreview.com)	DF	DF	DF	
Web	MSN MONEY (moneycentral.msn.com/home.asp)				
Web	MSNBC (www.msnbc.com)	DF	DF		DF
Web	NEWSDAY (www.newsday.com)	DF	DF	DF	DF
Web	NPR (www.npr.org)		(Selected Broadcasts) DF		(3 News Shows) DF
Web	NY POST (www.nypost.com)		DF		DF
Web	NYTIMES (www.nytimes.com)	DF	DF	DF	DF
Web	PBS (www.pbs.org)		(Charlie Rose show only) DF		
Web	PR NEWSWIRE (www.prnewswire.com)	DF	DF	DF	DF
Web	RED HERRING (www.redherring.com)	(Abstracts) DF		DF	DF
Web	REUTERS (www.reuters.com)		DF		
Web	SALON (www.salon.com)				
Web	SALT LAKE TRIBUNE (www.sltrib.com)	DF	DF		
Web	SAN JOSE MERCURY NEWS (www.mercurynews.com)	DF	DF	DF	DF
Web	SEARCH ENGINE WATCH (www.searchenginewatch.com)				
Web	TECHNEWSWORLD (www.technewsworld.com)				
Web	TIMES ONLINE (www.timesonline.co.uk)	DF	DF		DF
Web	TORONTO STAR (www.thestar.com)	DF	DF	DF	DF
Web	USA TODAY (www.usatoday.com)	DF	DF	DF	DF
Web	VENTUREWIRE (www.venturewire.com)				
Web	WASHINGTONPOST.COM (www.washingtonpost.com)		DF	DF	DF
Web	WIRED NEWS (www.wired.com)				

Type	Title	Dialog: NewsRoom	Factiva: Track	Intelligance Data: InSite 2	LexisNexis Personal News*
Web	WORLD PRESS REVIEW (www.worldpress.org)	(Abstracts) DF	DF	DF	
Web	YAHOO! NEWS (dailynews.yahoo.com)				
Web	ZDNET (www.zdnet.com)		(U.K., FRENCH AND GERMAN VERSIONS) DF	(Various ZDNET print pubs) DF	(FRENCH VERSION) DF

* Depending on the specific LexisNexis database accessed, some titles are available in full text, others in summary/abstract form. We have noted "abstracts" only when no databases offer the title in full text.

The *Tools* For Tomorrow...

Today!

KMWORLD

KMWorld serves the information needs of business executives and departmental directors who leverage the various forms of business content to improve their day-to-day business processes. Focusing on content, document, and business knowledge management, *KMWorld* provides actionable information through real-world case studies, advice from key practitioners, and best-practice advice from market leaders. Subscription in the U.S. is free to qualified corporate executives who complete an electronic online subscription application form at *www.kmworld.com/subscribe*. For corporate libraries and non-qualified recipients, the annual subscription price is $63.95 U.S., $86 Canada & Mexico, and $116 Outside N.A. in U.S. funds and prepaid upon application.

COMPUTERS IN LIBRARIES

Computers in Libraries provides the most complete coverage of library information technology. Every issue contains articles on library automation, online products and services, the Internet, CD-ROM/multimedia, document delivery, and much more! *Computers in Libraries* delivers clear, useful advice and ideas written by and for library professionals. 10 issues/yr. 1 yr. $99.95 U.S., $114 Canada & Mexico, $124 Outside N.A.

SEARCHER

Searcher: The Magazine for Database Professionals is a unique publication that explores and deliberates on a comprehensive range of issues important to the professional database searcher. *Searcher* contains evaluated online news, searching tips and techniques, reviews of search aid software and database documentation, and trenchant editorials, along with many topics of interest to the experienced database searcher. 10 issues/yr. 1 yr. $83.95 U.S., $107 Canada & Mexico, $113 Outside N.A.

ECONTENT

EContent magazine clearly identifies and explains emerging digital content trends, strategies, and resources to help professionals navigate the content maze and find a clear path to profits and business processes. *EContent* is the most reliable source for what matters in electronic content, the content infrastructure, and the business of digital content. 10 issues/yr. 1 yr. $112 U.S., $122 Canada & Mexico, $147 Outside N.A.

CRM

CRM magazine is the leading publication serving the field of customer relationship management. *CRM* is a business technology magazine written for senior level management in corporate, sales, marketing, service, and information technology and provides business leaders with the information they need to reach their strategic objectives through tactical implementation of CRM process and technology. *CRM* magazine is free to qualified subscribers who complete an electronic online subscription application at *www.destinationcrm.com*.

INFORMATION TODAY

Information Today is the newspaper for users and producers of electronic information services. *Information Today* provides complete coverage of online databases, the Internet, CD-ROM products, multimedia, library automation, electronic networking and publishing, and the essential hardware and software for delivery of electronic information. 11 issues/yr. 1 yr. $69.95 U.S., $93 Canada & Mexico, $102 Outside N.A.

For more information or to subscribe call **(800) 300-9868**; outside the U.S. call (609) 654-6266.
Visit our Web site at *www.infotoday.com*; or e-mail: *custserv@infotoday.com*
Write to: **Information Today, Inc.**, 143 Old Marlton Pike, Medford, NJ 08055